What's Your Story?

WHAT'S YOUR STORY?

A Young Person's Guide to Writing Fiction

Marion Dane Bauer

Clarion Books
New York

Clarion Books
a Houghton Mifflin Company imprint
215 Park Avenue South, New York, NY 10003
Text copyright © 1992 by Marion Dane Bauer

Printed in the U.S.A.

Library of Congress Cataloging-in-Publication Data
Bauer, Marion Dane.
   What's your story? : a young person's guide to writing
fiction / by Marion Dane Bauer.
     p.   cm.
   Summary: Discusses how to write fiction, exploring such
aspects as character, plot, point of view, dialogue, endings,
and revising.
   ISBN 0-395-57781-0
   1. Short story — Juvenile literature.   2. Fiction —
Authorship — Handbooks, manuals, etc. — Juvenile literature.
3. Children as authors.   [1. Fiction — authorship.
2. Creative writing.]
I. Title.
PN3373.B25   1992
808.3'1 — dc20   91-3816
                                                          CIP
                                                           AC

BP 10 9 8 7 6 5 4 3 2 1

For my editor,
James Cross Giblin,
with affection and appreciation,
because every story I write
is deeper, truer, stronger
for passing through his hands

Contents

Introduction / ix

1. The First Step . . . A Story Plan / 1

2. Choosing Your Best Idea / 8

3. Character . . . The Key to Good Stories / 17

4. Bringing Characters to Life / 28

5. Focusing Your Story / 37

6. Getting from Beginning to End . . . The Plot / 46

7. Choosing Your Point of View / 57

8. At Last . . . The Beginning / 68

9. Something to Talk About . . . Dialogue / 78

10. Story Tension . . . Keeping Your Readers Hooked / 87

Contents

11. Endings . . . Expected and Surprising / 95
    12. Just When You Thought You Were
        Done . . . Revising / 102
    13. The Final Step . . . Polishing / 111
    14. A Career as a Fiction Writer / 118
An Afterword . . . On Using This Book / 127
        Index / 131

Introduction

We are born hungry. We are hungry for food, for warmth, for a loving touch, and for something else as well. We are hungry to understand, to make sense of the world around us. Almost as soon as we begin to talk, we ask a single question, over and over again. "Why?" And we are still asking that same question when we say, only slightly later, "Tell me a story."

Human beings are storytelling animals. That's what separates us from other creatures, not just having thumbs or using tools.

Stories help us to make sense of our world. They teach us what is possible. They let us know that others before us have struggled as we do. If Hansel and Gretel can escape the wicked witch, so can we. If the poor prince is rewarded for his kindness, then we might be, too.

So from an early age, we begin to shape our own world by telling stories ourselves. "I'll be the mother and you be the father and this is our house and . . ."

Or, "Once upon a time, there was a boy who *hated* his little sister. It wasn't me. It was some other boy who had a little sister." Our stories put us in charge. They allow us to explore our feelings without having to face the consequences of acting them out. They help us understand what it means to be a human being.

Creating stories is important work for the professional writer. It is as important as building highways or selling shoes or making laws. And we each have our own stories to tell, whether we are professional writers or not. Even when we are very young — perhaps especially when we are very young — stories bubble inside us. When we share them with others, we discover that they are usually eager to hear them.

Where do storytellers find the wisdom to discover their own stories, the ones others are longing to hear? From no place more mysterious than their own hearts. Thus, the first thing we must know before we can begin to write a story is ourselves. We don't need to understand every crevice and corner. No one ever does, no matter how long we live. But we must understand some of our own truths. What ideas excite us? What makes us laugh . . . or cry? What are we struggling to understand?

Learning to tell a good story is hard work. Learning to write one, refining our words for an audience we will never see, is harder still. It's at least as hard as learning to ski or to play a musical instrument. But writing stories can be the kind of work that makes us glad to be alive. It stretches our mental muscles and leaves us feeling excited and proud. It can be work we love to do.

You'd love to write a story? Wonderful. Let's begin.

The First Step . . . A Story Plan

Many people want to write stories. Many more people want to write them than ever get around to doing it. That is partly because stories take time. They take time to grow in the author's mind, time to write down, and time to rework until they are ready to be read.

Everyone's day has the same number of hours. If you want to do something special like writing a story, you must make time just for that. And making time usually means taking it from some other part of your life. Turn off the television set. Practice writing thirty minutes a day instead of playing the marimba. Organize your homework or your bedtime ritual more efficiently. A story isn't a gift delivered while you are thinking about something else. It is a project you will need to work on with thought and care.

Thus, the first part of creating a story plan is making a plan for yourself. When will you write? Where? How often? For how long? Choose a time that is regular and one that is right for you. Are you going to set your alarm early and work from five to seven A.M. every day? Unless you are a very unusual person, such a plan probably won't last beyond the first morning. Decide what is realistic for you. Ask yourself, also, how much writing time you can enjoy. Thirty minutes a day? Fifteen? Two hours on weekends? Then make story writing a pleasant habit in your life.

If you find yourself brushing the cat or even offering to wash the dishes during the time you've set aside for writing, reconsider. Do you really want to write a story, or do you want to *have written* one? The two are very different.

But, you say, you *do* want to write a story. Then begin by finding a place in your life where writing time fits, comfortably and regularly, like practicing the piano or pressing weights. And then make that time work for you. You will achieve far more by writing fifteen minutes a day than you will by waiting for that mythical future when you are going to have nothing else to do.

What Is a Story?

We all have read hundreds of stories and have had them read to us as well, probably since we were very small. However, most of us can feel what a story is better than we can explain it. Creating something that matches this feeling can be difficult.

Let's try this definition: A story, any story, is about someone struggling. The main character must have a problem he has to struggle to solve, or he must want something he has to struggle to get. If there is no struggle, there is, quite simply, no story.

(The term that is often used for this struggle in fiction is *conflict*. I prefer the word *struggle,* because the idea of struggle implies that the main character is active. Too many stories by beginning writers fail because they have a main character who is passive in the face of a conflict.)

The definition I have given fits the shortest short stories and the longest novels. The difference between the two lies in complexity and, of course, length. Much of what I will be discussing fits either, but most writers begin with short stories. They are more manageable for learning on.

For one thing, if you begin by working on short stories, you can have the satisfaction, and the good experience, of *finishing* many different ones. New writers who launch into a novel often get lost along the way and never finish even one.

For another, the short story is simpler; the characters are fewer and the story lines clearer. As you work on a shorter piece, it will be much easier to keep track of the different parts.

So even though I will sometimes give examples from my own novels — and even though most of what I will say applies equally to novels — this guide is designed primarily to help you plan and write a short story.

A Writer's Notebook

The core of any story plan is an idea that involves someone struggling toward something. Sound simple? It is. However, if you asked me to come up with an idea for a new story right now, I would probably be pretty blank. And the more anxiously you waited for results, the blanker I would be apt to feel. What I need in this early stage, and what you will need as well, is time. Time to think, to remember, to observe.

There is a problem, however, with setting aside a day or a week or a month to *think* about something. Too often, we go about our lives and forget to do much thinking.

A writer's notebook helps with this problem. Get one small and light enough to carry with you. Have it beside you at the breakfast table, in school, when you go to a movie. Put it next to your bed at night. Make it a presence in your life, a constant reminder to be thinking about someone struggling toward a solution to a problem.

A spiral notebook is a good kind to choose. They are inexpensive and easy to find. The style stenographers use has a firm cover that gives a good writing surface, even when you want to make notes on the bus. And you won't be apt to lose pages out of it.

Who? What?

At the top of the first page of your notebook write two questions to remind yourself of what you're doing. *Who is the story about?* and *What does he want?*

When an idea comes to you — from something in your own life, a newspaper story, television, school, a conversation overheard at the mall — jot it down in your notebook. You don't need to write it out fully or to write so anyone else can understand it. Put down just enough to prompt your memory when you check your notes later.

The possibilities are endless, and now is not the time to limit them. Just keep making notes whenever you have an idea. Remember that each character you think about must be involved in a struggle. Deciding only that your story is going to be about a chimpanzee or about a sixteen-year-old boy doesn't reveal much. You must know what that character wants.

There are many desires that either a chimp or a teenage boy could have. The chimp could be in love with an alligator. The boy might need a good grade on a chemistry test. Or he could want to stop his mom from drinking. Or he could get lost in the woods on a camping trip and need to find his way back to his friends.

Perhaps the branch tapping against your bedroom window on windy nights makes you think of ghosts. Jot down *ghosts at a bedroom window at night*. Then you need to decide, Whose story is it? Who has the problem to solve? The person in the room, or the ghost? The decision is yours, because it can be either one. Perhaps you will want to consider both stories, the human being's and the ghost's.

If you decide your story belongs to the person in the room, then who is he and what does he want? The first and most obvious answer is that he wants to drive the ghost away. You can certainly base a story on someone trying to do just that.

But perhaps your main character is a woman who has always wanted to meet a ghost. Then you have another story entirely. Or it might be a boy who absolutely refuses to believe in the existence of ghosts. Maybe he wants to prove there is some rational, scientific explanation for the noise at the window.

If you want to explore the story from the ghost's point of view, then return to the same question. Who is the ghost? What does he want? This might be a vampire ghost, growing weak for lack of fresh blood. Or it might be a ghost who is afraid of the dark and is trying to get into the light and warmth of the room. Or it might be a neighbor playing tricks!

Don't stop there. After you have made notes about every angle of the ghost story you can think of, move on to other ideas. When it comes time to choose the story you want to write first, you can never have too many ideas to draw from.

Maybe there is a new girl in school who everyone thinks is stuck-up. What is her story? What might she want? To move back to the place she came from? To be accepted by the students in her new school? Is acting stuck-up a way of covering her fear? You probably can't *know* the answers to any of these questions about the real girl, but you don't need to know. You can make up whatever your story needs.

A television documentary about the slaughter of dolphins might catch your attention. Make notes about a dolphin carried off in a tuna net. Or perhaps the dolphin's dilemma sets you to imagining the plight of other creatures. A Canada goose during hunting season. What is the goose's problem? Has a hunter shot his mate? Does he want revenge? Does he want the hunter to shoot him, too? Does he want to warn the other geese?

The documentary on the dolphins might even get you thinking about ways humans can hurt one another. A boy set upon by a pack of bullies, for instance. Why would the bullies attack him? How can he fight back? Is there any way he can defeat the whole gang . . . or even confront the gang and survive?

Jot down your thoughts as they come without worrying if an idea is "good" or "bad." Simply write down every story idea you think of. Keep your notes brief. You are not writing your story yet. You are gathering ideas for as many different stories as possible.

Give yourself time with this process, at least a week. But use the time fully. Don't set yourself a deadline and then forget about the whole thing until the night before. Story ideas come hard under such last-minute pressure.

Most of all, have fun with your search for ideas. You often must write letters and reports and themes to please other people. The first and best reason for writing stories is to please yourself. Besides, a story you enjoy writing is likely to be one your readers will enjoy reading.

At its best, story writing is an art. And when you are dealing with art, any kind of art, your pleasure in making it is what matters most.

Choosing Your Best Idea

You have been gathering story ideas for days now. You're getting so you can't turn out a light without imagining a story about a blackout. Your mother hands you a bowl of oatmeal, and you see a mother rabbit serving up carrot porridge . . . to the only rabbit child in history who can't stand carrots!

The process you have begun is one that will stay with you the rest of your life. Or it will if you are serious about being a fiction writer. You have begun to see the world as something to shape and direct and control. You have begun to discover and create stories.

You probably have ideas jotted down for at least half a dozen different stories by now. But of course, no one can write half a dozen stories at once. Almost certainly, too, some of your ideas will make better stories than others. So the next step is to choose the story you want to work with.

Sorting Your Ideas

At this point, there are three basic questions that will help you choose your most effective story ideas. Examine each situation you have considered and ask yourself these questions:

1. Can your main character solve her own problem? If someone else has to solve the problem, then the story belongs to that other person. A boy who wants to be on the school baseball team had better be able to make it on his own (or decide for himself that he would rather do something else). If his father must talk the coach into giving the boy a chance, then it is really the father's story. He is the one struggling to resolve the problem.

If, on the other hand, no one can solve the problem, then you have a situation, not a story. Stories require solutions. In fact, that is one of the ways in which stories are different from our everyday lives. Many of the problems we live with are never really solved, or the solution comes so gradually we hardly notice. We turn to stories because they give us a feeling of resolution that is often missing in our lives.

In real life, a pesky younger brother may well grow up to be a pleasant man and a good friend. That doesn't help much right now, though. In a story, a girl with such a brother needs to solve her problem in some way. And she needs to solve it in the present, not in the future.

Maybe she devises a cage for her brother and convinces him that he is a lion in a zoo. Then she can have her friends over for a slumber party while "the lion" watches happily from a distant corner. This is an example of a story in which a character changes her situation.

There is another way in which story problems are often solved. The main character may change herself instead of her situation. The girl might slip away, leaving her pesky brother alone in a park . . . only to discover later that he hasn't found his way home. She would search for him, feeling guilty and worried. And she would be so relieved to find him that she would change her attitude toward him. She would decide she is glad to have him around.

Or let's return to the chimp that was mentioned earlier, the one in love with an alligator. She might change her situation. For example, she could get what she wants by marrying her alligator. Or she might change herself. After several dangerous attempts to get close to the alligator, she could decide she would be happier with another chimp.

Some of the story situations you jotted down in your notebook may require someone other than the main character to solve them. Other story ideas may have no solution at all, either through the main character's changing the situation or through his changing himself. Cross those off, and go on to the next questions.

2. Will your main character have to struggle to solve his problem? Remember, it is the struggle (or conflict) that makes the story. What if I told a story this way:

There was a girl who wanted to have a slumber

party, but she was afraid her pesky younger brother would ruin it. So she decided to have her party at a friend's house instead.

Or:

There was a chimp who fell in love with an alligator. She went to the alligator and said, "Will you marry me?" The alligator said he would and the two lived happily ever after.

What would you say? BORING! Of course, because both solutions are too easy. If your story is to be interesting, your main character must struggle against real difficulties to obtain what she wants.

Review your ideas, and cross off any that won't require a real struggle.

3. Is the problem important to the main character? This doesn't mean your story situation needs to affect the entire world (nuclear war or the destruction of rain forests). Nor does it have to threaten anyone's life. In fact, it doesn't need to matter at all except to the person who has the problem — your main character.

However, the problem must be genuinely significant to that character or your story won't feel important to the reader. You could write a story about a girl wanting a new dress. But her reasons for wanting the dress (and the difficulties keeping her from getting it) would need to be very important to her.

Perhaps a particular kind of dress is required for acceptance into a club the girl wants to join. And maybe her parents refuse to let her have one like it, saying it isn't appropriate for a girl her age.

Or she might find a dress in a store that, before her very eyes, transforms her into her sister, the one she has always envied and admired. But she doesn't have enough money to buy it.

Check the ideas remaining on your list. Ask yourself why your main character cares about his problem. You might decide that a dog wants to take off his fur coat because he thinks it makes him ugly. And he is afraid that he is too ugly to be adopted. Or maybe a boy who dislikes playing hockey feels he must try out for the team to win his girlfriend's approval.

Don't be too quick to decide that a problem isn't important. Ask yourself why your character cares, and you will probably find a reason. If you don't, however, you can cross that story idea off your list.

After you have answered these questions, you should still have several ideas left to choose from. If you don't, go back to your original process and gather more ideas; then run them through the three questions again.

Choosing the Idea Best for You

Answering the questions we have just discussed will help you choose those ideas that can make good stories. There is still something more to think about, though. Writing a story takes time and thought and energy. You want to spend that time and thought and energy on a story idea that is right for you.

So the next check is with yourself. Does your story idea feel as important to *you* as it does to your main character? After all, where are you going to discover your main character's strong feelings if not in yourself?

The easiest test I know for picking your best idea is to put your notebook aside and go about your life. Which story ideas stay with you? Which ones keep coming back, rolling like a snowball, with more bits of story attached every time? Which ones make you feel excited?

That excitement is the real test of a good story idea, an idea that is good for *you*. You may not know why one idea seems more important to you than another. And knowing why doesn't really matter. In the process of writing your story, there is a good chance you will discover where in your own life your idea comes from. But to write it, you need only be able to feel the excitement, not to explain it.

None of this means that you will limit yourself to writing about things that actually happened to you. I know that if I limited my stories in such a way, I would have few to tell. The point to remember is that you can't expect your stories to be important to your readers if they aren't important to you first.

What If . . . ?

If you find yourself confining your ideas too closely to the realities of your everyday life, you will need to learn to do some story stretching. Few of us live lives that, taken whole, provide more than very occasional material for stories.

You can move beyond the confines of your own experience in one simple step, however. Learn to ask yourself, What if . . . ?

Begin with an experience, an idea, a feeling important to you, and then make it entirely new with that simple question. What if my father hadn't found me that time I got lost in the department store? What if a girl as ordinary as I am got kidnapped by space invaders? What if a big, burly policeman was afraid of dogs, even little ones, the way I am?

Perhaps you find it easy to do well in school. Maybe you have never been tempted to cheat. But what if you were suddenly confronted with a subject you didn't understand no matter how hard you tried? Thinking about that, can you understand the panic of the boy who thinks he must cheat to pass chemistry?

Or maybe your parents seem terribly overprotective. It seems as though they will never let you do anything or go anywhere. In that case, you might feel real empathy for a zoo bear who wants to travel.

The question What if . . . ? allows you to create stories that go far beyond anything that has ever happened to you.

In my novel *A Dream of Queens and Castles,* Diana has been forced to move to England with her mother. She resents the move and wants to be with her friends at home. I never experienced such a problem. My family moved only once in all the years I was growing up, and that was from one side of a cornfield to the other. The move changed little in my world. And while I did live in England for a year as an adult, I didn't go with Diana's reluctance.

I have, however, moved often as an adult. I also have had the experience, when I was about Diana's age, of changing schools. I found going into the new school extremely difficult. So I could understand, I could actually feel, Diana's reluctance to take on this new place.

My year of living in England gave me the experience of being an American there. (Notice, I didn't use an English girl for my main character. I know too little of what it would be like to grow up in England.) I combined that experience with my painful memory of changing schools. What I came up with was a girl who was being forced to move. Only her move wasn't merely to a new school. It was to a new country.

The secret is to find that place within yourself where feelings are strong and then to ask, What if . . . ? What if a boy who loved football as much as you do sprained his wrist before the big game? What if there was a chipmunk who got scared in tight, dark places . . . the way you do?

A Surplus of Riches

Story ideas are everywhere, in every person you know, in every situation you meet. There is, perhaps, a story idea in your next visit to the dentist. Has he been taken over by alien beings who are mining human teeth? Is he growing rich robbing people's mouths? How can a patient stop him from pulling all her teeth? Can the dentist be rescued from his alien possession?

What about the old woman who walks past your house every day, always staring at the sidewalk? Is she looking for something? What? A ring she once lost, perhaps? Who gave her the ring? Her long-dead hus-band? Or is it a magic ring that will make her young again?

People often say, "I'd love to write a story, but I wouldn't know where to begin." Well, we've seen how you can begin. Think of someone who must struggle to resolve a problem. Decide what she wants. Test your idea to make sure your character can solve her own problem and that the solution won't be too easy. And then check the whole thing against your own feelings. Does the idea excite you? Do you really care about what your character will be going through?

Finally, if your story follows your own life too closely, stretch it by asking, What if . . . ?

When you have done all that, you have the beginnings of a story. Now it's time to consider another question. Who are these people in your story?

Character . . . The Key to Good Stories

Some stories we read, or watch on television or at the movies, and then forget almost as soon as we are done. Others seem to take hold of us, to become a part of our own lives. The difference between them has little to do with the excitement of the story action. (How many car chases have you watched on film, probably without being able to remember a single one in detail?) Rather, it depends much more upon how interesting, believable, and unique the characters are.

Good stories stand or fall on good characters. Every fiction writer needs to learn to create characters who will live in readers' hearts.

You already have the beginnings of a character for the story you have decided to write. You have answered two basic questions about her: Who is she, and what does she want?

However, if you know only that much, she will be a stick figure moved by your plot. Stick figures are easily forgettable. So next you need to learn to build characters who will come alive and take charge of their own stories.

Most characters begin in the author's mind with a simple stereotype. Freckled, mischievous, ten-year-old boy. Grumpy bear. Popular, pretty cheerleader. Shy mouse. Such a simple beginning is fine. And you probably imagined a stereotype automatically when you were first deciding on your story problem.

A stereotype, however, describes only the most obvious surface. It is what we see at first glance, what we assume about people whom we don't know. And it hides as much as it reveals. If your characters remain stereotypes, your readers won't care any more about them than they do about strangers glimpsed in a crowd.

Motive: The Key to Character

Understanding motive is the key to moving beneath the surface of the stereotype your character probably began as.

Return to your writer's notebook and to the story plan you have chosen to work with. Now is the time to ask a third question: Why does your main character want what she does?

The answer to that question is the force that will move your entire story. Motive.

For instance, you might have decided to write about a thirteen-year-old boy. What he wants is to join a gang of older boys. But why does he want to be part of that particular group?

The easiest way to find out is to hold an imaginary

conversation with him. Ask him questions, and let him answer in his own voice. Write his answers in first person; that means you will write as though your character is speaking, letting him refer to himself as *I*. There is no need to write the questions, only the answers.

Begin with the most obvious question, *Why do you want to get in with this gang?* In your imagination, what might this boy say? "I want to be part of the Chiefs because they're tough. Nobody pushes them around." That gives you an important piece of information. The boy wants to be tough. Maybe he is afraid of someone. And it also leads you to your next question. *Is somebody pushing you around?* Perhaps your character will answer, "There's these two guys, see? And sometimes when I'm walking home from school, they're laying for me."

Each piece of information your character gives leads to more questions. *What do they do when they catch you? How would the Chiefs protect you? What do you have to do to be part of their gang?* Let your character tell you anything he likes. Let him act — and react — as he will. When you begin writing in his voice, you may be surprised at what you discover.

Or perhaps the answer you get to your first question will be a very different one. Maybe your character wants to get in with this gang "because they're cool, the kind of guys the girls like." Then you might ask, *Is there some particular girl you want to like you? Who is she? Why do you think she would notice you if you were part of the Chiefs?* Whatever the answers are, each one will lead to other questions.

It's a little like getting someone to start talking and

then sitting back to listen. Each time he runs out of things to say, ask another question to get him going again.

As you do this, you will begin to feel as though you are two different people, the writer asking the questions and your main character himself. This dual role is one you will play throughout the entire process of writing your story.

History: The Key to Motive

Understanding your main character's history is the key to understanding her motives.

Whatever has happened to us in the past affects what we want today. A teenage girl whose father never paid much attention to her might want to date older men. Or a pampered young elephant might want a short nose because her mother never taught her the usefulness of her trunk.

In my novel *Face to Face,* the main character, Michael, wants two very different things. He wants to see his father again and to have his own .22 rifle. Both of these desires have a history. Michael hasn't seen his dad for many years and feels responsible for his having gone away. And Michael wants the gun because he remembers a time when he and his dad went deer hunting. The two desires intertwine in Michael's history and all through the story. And it is these past events that shape Michael's character . . . and consequently his behavior when he is confronted by the story problem.

Your character needs a history that relates very directly

to his struggle. When you are asking questions, ask about the past as well as the present. What happened before now to make her want what she does? Is there something from her past that makes her problem more important to her? Or more difficult to solve?

Perhaps a girl who wants a college scholarship comes from a family in which no one else has ever finished high school. Why haven't they? How do her parents and brothers and sisters feel about her going on to college? What is it about her past life that she wants to change through getting more education?

A china horse may have spent years shut inside a small box, as Moonseeker did in my fantasy novel, *Touch the Moon*. When he comes to life, he will still remember that dark, closed place and be afraid of being confined.

A girl might have moved many times with her professor mother . . . and only recently have had a chance to settle in and make friends. This is Diana's history in my novel *A Dream of Queens and Castles,* and it is the reason she is so displeased with the move to England.

You cannot know your characters without knowing some important points of their history. At the very least, you must know the background of the problem your main character will struggle with during the course of your story.

Name

So far we have been working with your character's insides, but there are external kinds of information that are important, as well. A name is one of the first things we learn upon meeting someone. So if you haven't yet given your main character a name, now is the time.

I find that my characters don't become fully real to me until I have named them.

You are free, of course, to choose any name you like. However, feel the fit of the name you choose. *Reginald Seymour Throckmorton III* gives us a particular image. *Butch Bates* gives another one entirely.

Avoid using the name of anyone recognizable, past or present. You can't call a character Benjamin Franklin or Marilyn Monroe without making people think of the real person. I avoid using the names of people in my own life, as well, because the person whose name I borrow begins to get in the way of the character I am creating.

You may already know what you want to name your character. If you don't, try a book of names or a telephone directory for ideas. Pay attention to the sound of names, to their rhythm and length. Notice the way first and last names fit together.

Also, think about the way different characters' names work with one another. I give my characters names that begin and end with distinctly different sounds. I try for different lengths and rhythms, as well. This helps the reader keep my characters straight. (Have you ever read a story in which two characters have very similar names, such as Stacy and Tracy, or Bob and Bill? Perhaps you found yourself struggling to remember who was who. You don't want your readers to have to struggle in that way.)

Appearance

Next, decide what your main character looks like. If you are like me, your first attempt will prompt you to come up with something pretty general. Brown hair/brown eyes. However, brown hair/brown eyes could fit millions of people, each of whom is unique.

The key isn't to describe a character in detail, every part from head to toe. If you do that, you are probably telling more than your reader wants to know. It also takes a lot of your story time to do it. Instead, the key is to find some small aspect of the appearance of each of your characters that sets the person apart. How would you describe your character if someone had to pick him out in a room full of people?

Perhaps a girl has a pert, turned-up nose like a pug dog. Or a man wears trousers that ride below his round belly. A boy might have a cowlick standing like an exclamation mark on the crown of his head. Or an old woman's hand gripping her cane could look like a claw.

Some writers go through newspapers and magazines and cut out photographs of people to populate their stories. If that idea appeals to you, put the photos in your notebook, where you can refer to them often. However, you'll need to choose pictures that look like real people. Many photographic models are too perfect to be interesting or believable as characters.

Study people. There is a lot to see as you walk down the street, move through your school halls, or even sit at your own supper table. Notice the lines that appear when someone frowns. A habit of pushing hair back from the face. Gnawed fingernails. Might your character look like that or do that? You can tell a lot about people's thoughts and feelings by examining their faces, the way they dress, the way they walk. It is important for you to know this kind of information about your characters, as well.

You might want to set aside a part of your notebook for descriptions of people you meet. Look at everyone, not just those who might fit this particular story. Remember, you have a lifetime of stories ahead of you.

Notice the elderly man fumbling with the clasp on his coin purse. Observe the way a little girl sucking her thumb continually brushes her nose with her index finger. Taking notes on such details will teach you to be observant. You can only show your readers what you have noticed yourself.

Environment

Your characters must live somewhere, and you will need to decide where. On this planet or on Mars? In this country or another? In a city or a suburb, a small town or on a farm?

If you are writing a fairy tale or science fiction, your setting probably needs to be imaginary. But for a realistic story that takes place today, it is easiest to choose a place you know. A solid, familiar setting will help make your story real.

After you choose the general environment, be more specific. What are your character's immediate surroundings like, especially that part he has created for himself.

Are you writing about a nine-year-old boy? Then what is his room like? Does he keep moldy peanut-butter-and-jelly sandwiches under his bed? A pet toad in his dresser drawer?

Or are you writing about a boy who has posters of rock stars covering his walls? Or one who spends his time in a basement laboratory doing scientific experiments? You will learn more about your characters as you make such decisions about their surroundings and jot down brief notes on them.

Secondary Characters

Your story will, in almost every case, need secondary characters in addition to your main character. One of the few stories that can be told with one character is that of a man (or woman) against nature. However, nature itself is almost a character in such a story. It is the opponent, and as such has a kind of personality: a harsh Arctic waste; a lush, tropical jungle; a searing desert. (Gary Paulsen's *Hatchet* is an excellent example of this kind of story.)

Usually, though, the conflict is with other people or another person. In fact, in most stories it is important for the main character to have a human opponent. His struggle with someone (an overly strict parent, a bully, a scary ghost) will help to keep the story active. A main character who sits around alone and thinks about his problem all the time isn't going to be very interesting.

There also may be people (or a person) who provide support for the main character. Not great crowds. Two or three secondary characters are all there's room for in most short stories. So, for example, there could be one person causing the problem for the main character, and another person helping her solve the problem.

Once you have decided who else is in your story, you will need to know more about them. Simply follow the same process with each secondary character that you did with your main character. However, make your notes in the third person (using *she* or *he*), and do not ask the characters to talk to you directly. That is because you won't be inside the secondary characters at any time in the story. Limiting yourself (and consequently your reader) to your main character's thoughts is an important way of focusing your story. Because your secondary characters won't be as important, you can develop them in less depth also.

In particular, though, decide what each character wants with regard to the main character's struggle.

Consider, for instance, a story about a mouse who wants to be king of the jungle. Who might the other characters be? Perhaps one would be the mouse's mother, who wants to see her son as king. And of course, there would be the lion who is going to have his position challenged. What does he want? To remain king? For someone else to have the burden and responsibility of ruling the jungle? Or maybe he is taking a nap, and he doesn't care who is king so long as he can go on sleeping.

Your secondary characters need names and environments and appearances just as your main character does. Their appearances may actually be more important to you than your central character's. That is because you will tell your story from your main character's point of view. Since you will be inside her, you won't be paying much attention to the way she looks unless appearance is part of your character's problem. But because your main character will be seeing the others in the story, the reader will need to see them, too.

Moreover, physical description can be a good device for summing up less important characters. What if I tell you that a little boy looks like a walking mud pie? Do you begin immediately to form an opinion about him? Or I might mention that a teacher has a hawklike nose and that he perches on the edge of his desk as if ready to pounce. How would you feel about being in his class? There's not much question, is there?

Remember, you are not yet writing your story. These are preliminary exercises, but they are exercises that will make your story strong and rich. The more you know about your characters, especially about what they want and why they want it, the more your readers will care about them . . . and your story.

Also, the more you know about your characters, the more fully you can bring them to life. And bringing your characters to life is what we will look at next.

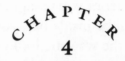
Bringing Characters to Life

Characters in stories are interesting because they seem like real people. Actually, no imagined person can ever be as complex as a living human being. However, if you and I create our characters well, our readers will be willing to pretend with us that they are real. They will even be willing to pretend that the imaginary problems these imaginary people struggle with are important.

You have already sorted out some parts of your characters' inner lives. You have asked what they want and why they want it. You have created a history for each person in your story. You have given them names, physical appearances, and an environment. The next step is to make your characters round, complex.

Creating complex characters will strengthen your story. It will also require more thought and planning. If you are growing impatient to move on, you may want to wait until you have had more experience before you concern yourself with this step. In any case, read through this chapter and take note of the ideas mentioned here. They may help even if you don't yet want to do the exercises suggested.

Writing fiction is something you learn in layers. Some of its secrets will open for you in writing this story; others will be revealed in years to come. For the rest of your life, every story you write will be an opportunity to learn more about creating fiction.

Defining Character Traits

In stories, as in life, people usually cause their own problems. Or if they don't cause them, then something about their basic personalities determines the significance the problems have for them.

Let's say your story centers around a girl who wants a new bike. By now, you have decided why she needs one. Perhaps she left her old bike lying in the driveway and her dad backed over it with the car. Now you need to ask a further question. What is it about the girl's personality that prompted her to leave her bike in the driveway in the first place?

Is she simply careless, the kind of kid who drops her bike without a thought?

Could she be good-hearted instead? Maybe she was trying to rescue a baby bird or running to tell her mother about a sick neighbor. She could have been so worried that she didn't notice where she left her bicycle.

Or perhaps she is someone who always wants to have the best, the newest, of everything. Maybe she doesn't care about her old bike any longer because it isn't the "in" style. Did she intentionally leave it to be ruined, expecting her parents to buy her a new one?

The problem in the story also may come entirely from the outside — a hurricane or an attack by a dragon, for example. If this is the case, the main character has nothing to do with actually causing the problem. However, an outside problem becomes far more interesting if the character must overcome something within himself to triumph over it. It is the human struggle we care about. Hurricanes and dragons without people trying to deal with them are pretty dull stuff.

To help you discover more about your character's personality and its relevance to the story problem, here are three questions to consider.

1. Why does your character have the problem he does? Is there something about his personality that causes — or at least contributes to — his problem? Does a girl steal homework from her schoolmate's desk because she wants to see the other girl in trouble? Or does she take it because she hasn't gotten around to doing her own work?

If the problem comes from outside, the hurricane or the dragon mentioned before, what prompted your character to be out in the hurricane or facing the dragon? Is he a brave knight trying to rescue a maiden, prove himself, get past the difficulty to some goal? Or is he a timid soul who was caught by the storm or the dragon while he was trying to flee danger?

2. What do you know about your main character

that will determine how she will react to the problem?   Is the girl jealous? Insecure? Lazy?

Is the knight terrified of storms or of fire? Is he a
blowhard who has always bragged of his strength or his
courage and now must prove himself at any cost? Is he
a quiet, confident person who will find his way around
the problem instead of confronting it head-on?

**3. Will facing the problem change your main char-
acter in any way?**   The jealous, insecure girl might
discover that the one she is jealous of is as vulnerable
as she. The lazy one might learn to organize herself so
she gets her own work done.

The knight who is afraid of fire might end up roasting
marshmallows at the dragon's mouth. Or the braggart
who wasn't bothered by storms might be quite humble
by the time this one passes.

Building in Contradictions

When you understand your main character's personality,
you will know how he will act throughout the story. A
greedy person would search for a treasure alone, hiding
his intent. A generous one would include others in the
search and the reward. However, if your character is
greedy (or generous) every moment of the story, he
won't seem real. He will be too predictable.

No one is the same all the time. We are filled with
contradictions. I am uncomfortable at big parties. Still,
I can give a speech to a thousand people without feeling

particularly nervous. I know a boy who acts tough much of the time. He acts like he doesn't care what anyone else thinks of him. Actually though, he is soft inside. The toughness is a cover for his fear of not measuring up to other people's expectations. Your characters, especially your main character, need some element of built-in contradiction, too.

The personality trait that triggers your story is the one the reader will be aware of most of the time. It will be the contradiction peeking through that will help to bring your characters to life.

At the moment when the bully shows he is frightened, we can understand and even care about him. The roaring monster becomes real when we see how lonely he is, how certain he feels that no one will ever like him.

In the first draft of my novel *Rain of Fire,* Steve, the main character, was a nice kid. That's about all anybody could say about him, he was *nice.* And he never changed at any moment. Somehow though, all his niceness didn't make him either believable or likable.

It was only in a second draft that Steve came alive. That was when I decided that he was also a liar. His lies didn't change his character particularly. In fact, it was his being a nice kid that prompted him to lie. He was trying to keep his friends and to protect his brother. But curiously, the contradiction in his personality made my readers like him better.

No one is totally good or totally bad. No one behaves in the same way in every situation and with every person, either. It is easy to forget the contradictions when you create characters. But a character who is all one way will be flat, boring, even unbelievable, to the reader.

The contradiction in the character may be hidden for a while. It often is. When it comes out, though, it might even help explain why your character acts the way he does. Is the bully afraid? Is the snob really shy? Does the popular girl who is always the center of a group feel as though she doesn't exist when she is alone?

Whatever contradictions you reveal in your character must relate to the way she deals with her problem. Knowing she is a dreamer won't help the reader if your story doesn't allow her to dream.

In the best fiction, every character will be complex. For now, though, concentrate on your main character. Learning to develop truly rounded characters takes time. I still work hard to do it with each of my stories and don't always succeed. But it is something worth striving for, starting with your very first story.

Where Do Characters Come From?

We have been through the entire process of building characters. We have begun with a simple stereotype and moved to complex beings who come alive on the page. But where are the ideas for these characters going to come from?

Partly from people you know, of course. All writers have to rely on their own experience of the world around them when they create characters. However, trying to put people into your stories exactly as you know them will probably lead you into difficulty.

In the first place, people you know aren't apt to behave on paper in ways your story demands. Your Uncle Bruce may insist on doing and saying only things you know he has actually done and said. That will limit your story, perhaps even stop it dead.

In the second place, your friends and family may not appreciate finding themselves in your stories.

And in the third place, however well you know other people, you can see them only from the outside. You must know your characters, especially your main character, from the inside.

There is, finally, only one person you know that way. Yourself. And what you know about yourself will be the primary material you will draw on for each of your characters. This is true even though they may be very different from you.

When I discovered that Steve didn't come to life in the first draft of *Rain of Fire,* I stopped to ask myself why. I realized, almost immediately, that I had given him nothing of my own inner experience. That was when, as I mentioned previously, I decided to make him a liar.

This doesn't mean that I ever told lies in the way Steve does. Actually, I have always been quite truthful in what I say. But when I was young, I was much less than truthful about what I wrote. Papers for school, letters to relatives, everything I put on paper became more interesting, more exciting, more meaningful, than the real event had been. I used to feel guilty about those lies I wrote. Still, storyteller that I am, I so much enjoyed writing them that I didn't seem to be able to stop.

When I thought about Steve, I knew exactly why he would lie. He would intend to tell the truth, but somehow the truth would never be quite good enough for his purposes. Giving him that piece of my own experience worked, even though his situation was very different from my own. In the same way, you can find pieces of yourself to share with your characters.

There is one basic question you will need to ask yourself over and over again: How would I feel?

This doesn't mean that every character you write about will be you. But it does mean that the only people you can write about well are those whom you understand. And we understand others through shared feelings. You can find that feeling connection with people who are unlike you in many other ways. They can be a different gender or a different age, or live a different kind of life.

Maybe you once had to stay in bed with a broken leg. That could help you understand the feelings of an old man who can no longer walk. It might prompt you, even, to understand a bird in a cage.

You don't need to come close to drowning to imagine how someone might feel being pulled underwater. You probably do need to have spent some time in the water, however. Then you can combine that knowledge with some other experience of fear.

It doesn't require wings to imagine flying. And you don't need to have been a horse to tell a story from a horse's point of view. However, you probably need to have known a horse or two if you want your story to be believable.

If you find you are having difficulty moving beyond the stereotype you began with, you may be working too far from your own experience. Perhaps no feeling of yours connects deeply enough with the character you are trying to write about. In that case, go back to your notebook and try another story idea, another character. Find one whose feelings you easily share. That will be your story and your person to write about.

Your own strong feelings can help you discover many, many characters and the stories they will live through.

A dozen different people, a hundred, already living inside of you? Exactly, and every one is waiting to find a home in the story only you can write.

Focusing Your Story

The next step I am going to suggest may surprise you. You have decided on the story problem your characters must struggle with. You know who those characters are, inside and outside. Now, before you can go any further, you need to decide exactly where your story is going to end.

Beginning to write a story without having your ending in mind is a little like starting on a trip without deciding where you want to go. Of course, you can start to drive, but how will you know when you have arrived?

Theme: What Does Your Story Mean?

Stories aren't simply entertainment, as people often suppose. Every story has a point or theme. It may have several, actually, but it will have one that is dominant. The theme isn't often stated. In better stories it almost never is. But it is clearly there. If you want to know what a story means, look first at the solution to the story problem.

Think of some of the classic stories you read when you were younger: "The Little Engine That Could," "Snow White," "The Pied Piper of Hamelin." The theme isn't stated in any of them. Still, it is obvious, isn't it?

How is it made clear? By the way the problem is resolved. The little engine gets to the top of the mountain by thinking positive thoughts, "I think I can. I think I can." If the little engine, despite all his positive thoughts, ended up in a wreck at the bottom of the mountain, the theme would be entirely different, wouldn't it? That is what happens in the Shel Silverstein poem "The Little Blue Engine" in *Where the Sidewalk Ends*. Mr. Silverstein even goes on to point out his theme that thinking you can just isn't enough.

In "Snow White," the wicked queen always gets the upper hand, despite Snow White's goodness, despite the love of the dwarfs. But love and goodness finally win out when the prince saves Snow White by kissing her. And the wicked queen, in her jealousy and fury, destroys herself because Snow White is "the most beautiful of all."

The obvious theme in "Snow White" is that love and goodness are "the most beautiful of all." A less obvious theme, because it is an idea taken for granted by our culture, is that every princess (woman) needs a prince (man) to "save" her.

In "The Pied Piper of Hamelin," because the people

of Hamelin fail to keep their promise to pay the piper for ridding their town of rats, they lose their children. That story says something very important about keeping promises, doesn't it?

In more complex stories, the theme may not be so obvious. It will still be there, however.

When you know the solution to your story problem, you will also know the theme or point of your story.

Consider, for instance, the story proposed earlier about the girl whose bicycle has been run over in the driveway. She wants a new one. There are any number of ways she might solve her problem.

Perhaps she could steal a bike and live with it happily ever after. If you solved her problem that way, what would your story be saying? "If you want something, take it," or "Crime pays." We don't have many stories with themes like that, because it's a message most of us don't accept. After all, we don't want anyone stealing *our* bicycles.

Or you could have the girl steal a bike, but then get caught. Or she could feel so guilty for taking it that she would decide to return it. If you ended the story in either of those ways, the theme would be one that is very common: "Crime doesn't pay."

She might work and work and work and finally earn enough money to buy herself a bicycle. The theme of such a story would be "Hard work brings rewards."

Perhaps she lost her old bicycle due to carelessness and has to work very hard to replace it. Then your last scene might show the girl riding her new bicycle home, starting to drop it in the driveway, but then reconsidering and wheeling it into the garage instead. In that case, the theme would be "We value what we earn by our own effort."

She could work to earn the money for the new bike but then decide to buy something her mother needs instead. The theme would be "The joy of giving is greater than the joy of having something for ourselves."

It isn't especially important that you be able to state your theme. Few writers do. And even if you can state it, you certainly won't want to stick it onto the end of your story. Fables come with morals tacked on like that. Other kinds of stories make their point through the story's action. It is crucial, though, that you understand your story's solution and what that solution means to you.

If you are going to have your character steal a bike and get away with it, then you had better believe in stealing. At least you had better believe in stealing in your character's circumstances. If you don't, you will probably have difficulty writing the story. You can tell what solution fits your story by deciding which one feels right to you. If it feels right to you, you will probably be able to make it feel right to your reader.

There are as many themes as there are people writing stories. And in fact, the themes of different stories may contradict one another. "Look before you leap" is the exact opposite of "He who hesitates is lost." One recommends caution; the other urges immediate action. "Love conquers all" is the opposite of "You always hurt the one you love." The first suggests that love solves all problems, the second that love itself is complicated and difficult. Each is true for different people in different circumstances.

Reading stories gives us a chance to understand the truths of other people's lives. Writing stories lets us share our own truths with others. It is important that your story come out of your own truth.

Discovering the Beginning in the Ending

Knowing how your story will end also helps you know exactly where it must begin. That is because the ending you intend will tell you what is important for the rest of the story. It will let you know what you want your reader to pay attention to from the first line on.

My novel *On My Honor* is about two boys, Tony and Joel, who go swimming in a forbidden river. Tony drowns. Joel, guilty and terrified, goes home without telling anyone what has happened.

In the first draft, the story began with Tony and Joel on their bikes heading down the hill toward the river. I soon discovered, though, that I didn't know what I wanted to say about the problem I had set up. And that was because I had a story problem — the drowning — that had no solution. So the only meaning my story could offer was something like "Isn't it terrible!" And that wasn't what I meant to say.

After some thought, I decided that I wanted the story to end with the moment when Joel finally confesses to his father. Knowing that, I realized that I had started at the wrong place. I needed to begin with a conflict between Joel and his father that Joel's confession would resolve.

So I began the story again, this time with Tony proposing that they bike out to the state park. Once there, he plans to climb some dangerous bluffs. Joel doesn't want to do the climb, but he also doesn't want Tony to think he's a wimp. So he turns to his father, expecting his father to rescue him by saying he can't go. Joel's father, however, doesn't understand what is at stake. He agrees to the trip, and Joel is furious with him from the first chapter. He even blames his father for Tony's death after it happens.

In the end, after Joel tells his father the truth, he feels close to his father again. He also realizes that he is responsible for his own decisions and that Tony was responsible for his. And finally, he understands that his father will be there for him, no matter what happens.

Knowing my resolution let me know my beginning. This approach will probably work for you as well.

A Circle or a Line

There are two common patterns for stories, as demonstrated by two different kinds of endings. One kind forms a circle, the other is a line.

On My Honor, which I have just been discussing, is a circle. In fact, most of my stories are circular. By the end, Joel has come back to the beginning. He is at home where he started. He is facing his father, whom he was facing at the beginning. And the story's resolution centers on how he repairs the connection with his father. That connection was broken at the story's opening, when his father failed to give Joel the "right" answer after he asked permission to ride out to the state park.

In a linear story the main character keeps moving forward until she gets what she wants. She will be in a very different place at the ending than she was at the beginning. "Cinderella" is an example of a story that makes a straight line. At first you think "Cinderella" is going to be a circle, that the main character is going to end up back in her cinders, but she doesn't.

Both kinds of endings are satisfying in different ways. The coming-home feeling of a circle, that moment when the end touches the beginning, is like a sigh. Seeing a character get what he wants in the linear story is like a victorious shout.

Finding Your Own Solution

You have already asked yourself whether or not your main character can resolve his own problem. Now it is time to decide what you want the resolution to be.

Let's examine another story mentioned earlier, the ghost who is afraid of the dark. What do you want to see changed by the end of the story? Do you want the ghost to have learned bravery? To convince some terrified human to protect him? Or to find a way so that he won't ever need to face the dark again? Each solution makes a different point. The trick is to find one that feels right to you — and to your main character.

When I was getting ready to write *Face to Face,* I

knew exactly how the story would end. Michael would come close to committing an act of terrible violence, then turn away from it. And I knew his acceptance of himself would save him from the violence.

Thus, my ending was clear in my mind, even though I wasn't sure in my first drafts what the violent act would be. In one draft, Michael held a gun on his family. In another, he lay in wait for a neighbor boy who had bullied him. Finally, with my editor's help, I decided that neither of those actions fit Michael. He would turn the gun on himself instead.

The true ending never changed, however. That is because the ending wasn't the near-violence of the climax. It was Michael's own resolution. It was his decision to put the gun aside and turn back to his family. (Another circular story.)

Thus, when I began writing, I knew where I was going. I knew what Michael's final moment would be and what it would mean. What he would do to get there I had to discover along the way.

Far more important than stating your theme is knowing your story's final moments before you begin to write, being able to feel them. Jot some ideas in your notebook about how you want your main character to solve her problem. You don't need to figure out yet all the steps that will take her to her solution, but you should know how the solution will feel.

Will your main character change his circumstances or himself? Will she be victorious in the end or defeated? Will he have made a new connection with another person or have turned away from him?

The ending you have in mind will express some part of your own individual vision of the world, your truth. Which means it must feel right to you. It must also feel important, satisfying. If it does, you are ready to move on to the next step, constructing your plot.

Getting from Beginning to End . . . The Plot

So what happens next? That's the question we ask on every page of a good story. It is the question you want your readers to be asking, too. But it can stump you as a beginning writer when you ask it about the story you are writing. If you don't know the answer, it is easy to decide that you aren't "creative" enough to write stories.

Fashioning a plot isn't as difficult as it might seem, though. Understanding the basic structure of most stories will help.

The Formula Story

The word *formula* has a negative sound to most people, at least as it applies to stories. However, there is nothing negative about using a formula to understand and control the structure of your story. Such stories can be as creative (or as uncreative) as those plotted by any other method.

The formula I am going to demonstrate is not the only way in which a story can be written, but it is the most common choice. Using this pattern is also the easiest way to write a successful story.

You know what your main character's problem is. You know where she will be after her problem is resolved. You know how that resolution will feel and, at least indirectly, what it will mean. Now for a further question: What will she do to solve her problem? It is your main character's continuing attempt to solve her problem that makes your story.

Return once more to the word *struggle*. Your main character must struggle. She can't solve her problem too quickly or there will be no story. However, she also can't go on struggling too long or the reader will lose interest.

If you're walking down a street and see a man scaling a tall building, you will probably stop to watch. His problem creates interest, and his struggle sustains tension. However, if he simply climbs the building, quickly and without difficulty, you will go on your way. You will probably even forget having seen him. At the other extreme, if it takes him hours and hours to get to the top, you will, most likely, lose interest after a time.

However, if he moves up steadily, but with obvious difficulty, you will probably stay to watch. If he moves steadily but falls back a couple of times on the way, you will be fascinated. The combination of his intense struggle and the real threat of his failure will hold you spellbound.

What I have just described is a pattern that is called the formula story when it is applied to writing fiction.

The Magic of Three

In the formula story, the main character often makes three attempts to solve her problem. Three is a satisfying number. In fact, it is a magic number. Think how many fairy tales involve three sons or give the heroine three wishes. Many of the other kinds of stories you grew up with use the number three in different ways, too. A few popular examples are "The Three Billy Goats Gruff," "The Three Little Pigs," and "The Three Bears." You can probably think of many more.

If you look at these stories closely, you will see that they use three to do more than just number the characters. Having three important characters sets the story up for three attempts to face the story problem. In "The Three Billy Goats Gruff," the troll challenges the goats three times . . . before being knocked off the bridge by the biggest goat. In "The Three Little Pigs," the big bad wolf makes three attempts to eat the pigs before he is finally foiled by the last pig.

In "The Three Bears," Goldilocks checks out three different items in the bears' house — the three bowls of porridge, the three chairs, and the three beds. Then each of the three bears checks out each of the three items as well before finding Goldilocks. So the story has threes upon threes upon threes.

How satisfying it always was to arrive at the final three. Remember the baby bear's cry, "And here she is!"

That is good storytelling, and the use of the number three is an important part of what makes it work.

You can make threes work for you as well. Have your main character try three times to solve her problem. The first two times she will fail. On the third, she will finally be successful. So the nonsense story about the chimp might go like this:

> *A chimp falls in love with an alligator. The problem is that the alligator isn't in love with the chimp. Perhaps he doesn't know she exists.*
>
> *1. So first the chimp sneaks up and leaves a bouquet of flowers. The alligator, not knowing what flowers are for, eats them.*
>
> *2. Next she decides that the poor alligator is hungry. So she brings bananas. The alligator tromps them into the mud.*
>
> *3. Finally, she presents herself, declaring her love. And the alligator, seeing her at last, falls in love, too.*

Or:

> *3. The chimp declares her love, and the alligator tries to eat her. So the chimp changes her mind. She goes to visit another chimp instead* (probably one who had been courting her in the beginning of the story), *carrying both flowers and bananas.* (In this case you have a circular rather than a linear story.)

Notice that in the first story plan, the chimp gets what she wants. That is the solution to the problem. In the second, she solves her problem by changing within herself. She changes her own mind about what she wants and decides to go after something else, or return to what she had in the beginning. Either way, the story is resolved on the third attempt.

Rising Action

There is something else to think about when you are planning your character's struggle. Each attempt must be stronger, more difficult to make, or more important than the one before. That's how you build the story tension.

Let's look at the chimp story again. How could you make each of those attempts stronger than the one before? Well, in this particular plot, the reader would worry about the chimp's safety. So on the first attempt you could have her leave the flowers and wait from the safety of the trees. That would worry the reader a little bit, but it would keep the chimp's risk low.

On the second, she could take the bananas and wait closer by to see the alligator eat them. That way the reader would worry more (and longer) about the chimp's safety. And of course, on the third attempt, we would worry even more about the chimp's actually presenting herself to the alligator.

Whatever your story, arrange the three attempts so the easiest comes first, the hardest last. Make each attempt increasingly important to the main character. Perhaps her danger becomes greater with each step, as we just plotted out. Or maybe she has only a limited time to solve her problem. (The alligator is engaged to marry another alligator, and she has to get his attention before the wedding takes place!) Or the problem simply may seem more important to her with each attempt; maybe she is getting more and more discouraged or increasingly frantic or more determined as the story progresses.

If you made a graph of a formula story, it would look like this.

The action increases in intensity (rising action) up to the first attempt, and then lessens (brief falling action) as the attempt fails. Then another rising action, even higher this time, occurs with the next attempt. That is again followed by a brief falling action. Finally, there comes a third rising action, rising higher than ever before with the third attempt. The character succeeds (or changes). Then there is a brief falling action that provides the reader with the last bits of information he needs in order to feel satisfied by the story.

Copy this graph into your notebook. That will help you keep the pattern in mind. Then make notes on or below the graph. What unsuccessful attempts might your main character make to solve his problem? How will he finally solve it? Think about how each attempt can be stonger, more difficult, or more important than the one before.

Notice, too, that this pattern focuses entirely on your main character's attempt to solve his problem. That struggle makes up the entire movement of your story.

You won't write about anything else. You can describe a sunrise if the sunrise sets the scene for what your main character is doing. You can include conversations with other characters if they, too, are involved in the story problem. But you won't include anything that isn't part of attempting to resolve the problem.

Staying with your main character's struggle to solve her problem will keep your story on track. Having the problem grow will build the tension in the story. And limiting the attempts to three will ensure that your story is neither too long nor too short.

Cause and Effect

It is possible, however, to follow the formula with care and still to write a fragmented story. Besides building in intensity, each event in your plot must lead, almost inevitably, to the next.

The following is not a plot:

> *A wicked queen doesn't like her stepdaughter. The stepdaughter goes to live with some little men in a forest. There she eats a poisoned apple and dies. A prince kisses her.*

One thing happens, then another, then another, but none of the events causes the next. Cause and effect is what holds a story together.

Think about the sequence of events in "Snow White," how each event causes the next one. The wicked queen is told that Snow White is more beautiful than she. Wanting to be the most beautiful in the land, she commands the hunter to take Snow White to the forest to kill her. The hunter, not liking the task, takes pity on Snow White and leaves her alive in the forest. Snow White, being left alone in the forest, stumbles upon the dwarfs' home. The queen, learning Snow White is still alive, sets out to kill her herself. And on the story goes, with each event making the next both possible and necessary.

Every part of your story should be an essential step along the way to the outcome. If a scene can be taken out without altering all that follows, it does not belong in your story.

Each attempt your main character makes to solve his problem should change something important for him. The change may be in outer circumstances. In *Rain of Fire,* Steve's attempt to cover his lie causes him to tell another lie, and so he gets into even deeper trouble. Or the change may be within the character entirely. In *Shelter from the Wind,* Stacy's helping with the difficult birth of the pups causes her to feel differently about the baby her stepmother is expecting. And her change of feelings makes her decide to go home.

It is not difficult to build this kind of cause and effect development if you look at each event through your main character's eyes. How will doing each thing change his circumstances? How will it change him?

When You Are Stuck

There will be times when you are planning or writing

a story that you will find yourself stuck. You cannot move your character forward another step. Trying to put down one word after another feels like slogging through quicksand. Perhaps you can't decide what you want to have happen next, or even if you know, you can't manage to get there.

I have had this experience many times, and somehow my years of writing don't seem to make it happen any less frequently. However, I have learned that my being stuck invariably comes from one of two sources.

The first is that I have lost track of my main character's struggle. He is no longer active. He is no longer trying to do something, to get somewhere. In that case, I must simply ask myself, What does he want now? Or, What is he doing to solve his problem?

The other reason for losing my forward momentum is that I have made a misstep earlier in the story. When I am really stopped in my tracks, the difficulty almost always begins some pages (or chapters) earlier than the point at which I became aware that something was wrong with my story.

So if your story quits moving, either in the planning or writing stage, ask yourself first if your character is still struggling. And if doing that doesn't get you moving forward again, then go back more deeply into your story. Has your character done something earlier that doesn't fit? Have you left out important action that is needed to get to this point? Have you gone off in a direction that doesn't lead to the ending you are aiming for?

Once you find the source of your difficulty, you may

have to take several more steps back. But don't ever be afraid to rethink and rewrite. When you are on track again, you will be rewarded for having had the courage to go back and make a fresh start. For then you'll probably find that you will sail past the place where you thought you were stuck.

Recognizing the Formula

It may sound as if stories written by the formula I have described would be too much alike to be interesting. But that isn't the case. There is room for great variety within this simple structure. The formula exists, in fact, because storytellers have always tended to use it, often without noticing they were following any kind of pattern at all. And they have used it because it works.

See if you can identify the pattern of the formula story in picture books and short stories. Novels, being longer, are more complex. They usually have subplots riding beneath and through the main character's struggle. Because of this, the formula pattern will rarely be as clearly visible in a novel. I find, however, that I often, quite unconsciously, use the pattern of the main character's making three attempts to solve some problem in individual scenes within my novels, especially action scenes.

You will be surprised at how often you can make out the framework of the formula story in stories you read. You will also, of course, find good fiction that creates its own patterns entirely. The best fiction often does.

But for beginning writers of any age, the formula story is usually the place to begin. Following its pattern gives you the greatest chance of creating a successful story . . . successful for your reader and for yourself as well.

Choosing Your Point of View

There is one final decision to make before you are ready to begin writing. It is quite a simple one, though essential. What point of view are you going to use for telling your story?

I am not asking which character you will use to tell your story through. I assume you will choose your main character, because that is usually the most effective way to present a story. There are some stories told through a lesser character, one who observes the main character's struggle. Those are for more experienced writers, though. It is hard to keep the reader caring about the main character through another person.

What I am asking is, Will you be writing your story in first or third person? In first person, the main character tells the story and refers to himself or herself as *I*. In third person, you tell the story and refer to your main character by name and as *she* or *he*.

First Person: Disadvantages

A story told in first person goes like this:

> *"I want to order a pizza," I said into the telephone, letting my voice quaver a little so I would sound like an old lady. "The biggest you've got."*
>
> *Kim was across from me, one hand over her mouth, practically choking on giggles.*
>
> *"Yeah . . . the extra large," I agreed. "That'll be fine." I gave Kim a dirty look. If she started me giggling, too, the guy taking the order was sure to get suspicious.*

(From my short story "Triple Anchovies")

Letting your main character tell your story seems easy. Writing in first person can feel as natural as writing a letter, as natural as talking: *I went downtown yesterday, and I saw . . .* But there are difficulties about working in first person that you should examine before choosing it.

1. Identifying the main character can be difficult when she is the one speaking. It can be hard even to let the reader know if the main character is male or female. (Notice that in my sample you aren't yet sure of that.) In third person, we have *she* or *he* and a name to let us know those things. In fact, in third person name and gender are both usually revealed from the first line.

One solution, of course, is to have your first-person

narrator introduce herself: *My name is . . .* That can be clumsy, though.

In my first-person novel, *Like Mother, Like Daughter,* readers can guess that the narrator is a girl in the first paragraphs. She complains about looking like her mother and talks about wanting to be different from her. These are strong clues. She also mentions a best friend named Kate, which helps as well. The reader doesn't know Leslie's name until the middle of the second page, however. That is when Kate says, "Leslie, did you see that?"

2. If your main character is telling the story, you must write in the character's voice, not your own. A person who is younger or older or different from you in some other way will affect the language you can use. You can't have a three-year-old say, *My older brother is simply obnoxious.* You also can't have a lion who lives in the wild comparing the moon to a streetlight. What would he know of streetlights?

3. Beginners writing in first person often *tell* the entire story and never get around to *showing* it or acting it out. A basic rule for fiction writers is: Show, don't tell. Those writing in first person have to work harder to stay with the action. Your reader doesn't want to hear about important events after they have happened. He wants to live through them. First person can be active, but having your character tell the story often makes it easy, too easy, to talk about the whole thing instead of letting the reader take part in the action.

4. When you are writing in third person, you can simply describe the environment along the way. If your character is telling the story, you have to create a reason for her to comment on the scene. I have found this easy to do when I move the character into a new location. It is more difficult when she is in her own town, her school, her bedroom. In a new location, we all look around, taking note of the way things are. Most of us take a familiar place for granted and quit seeing it — or at least quit commenting on it.

5. You may have difficulty deciding where your first-person narrator is in time. Have all of the story events already happened? If they have, will your narrator give away the ending before we get to it? Some writers have their narrators do just that — and intentionally. In such a story, the tension lies in finding out why something happened, not in what happened. This can be harder to carry off, though.

6. And finally, if the story's tension comes from worrying about whether the main character will survive, in first person the ending is given away. After all, he is still around to tell the story!

First Person: Advantages

Despite these problems, first person can work very well, for beginning writers or for professionals.

1. The readers feel immediately connected with the main character when he is telling his own story. The telling feels intimate. It is like hearing someone talk directly to you or like sharing a diary or letter. That is why romances are usually written in first person. A first-person voice can give the feeling of secrets shared.

2. A first-person story is often easier to believe than one written in third person. In third person, readers are always aware they are hearing a story. In first person, the narrator seems to talk directly to the readers. If he speaks in a convincing voice, readers will accept what they might ordinarily question. *It was a ghost (or a UFO)! I know, because I was there. I saw it!*

3. It is easy to reveal thoughts and emotions in first person. Your main character can simply tell what he is thinking and feeling:

> *I was so mad when she said that, I wanted to punch her lights out. At least I would have punched her lights out if she hadn't been a girl . . . and skinny and small and wearing braces on her teeth, no less. I mean, what can you do with somebody like that?*

4. The first-person voice gives you a chance to be funny (or philosophical). Your character can make whatever side comments fit his personality. My novels for young people are rarely funny, but *Like Mother, Like Daughter* uses a first-person narrator who is sometimes humorous.

The story begins like this:

> *The day I stood in the middle of a public park and watched my mother giving artificial respiration*

to a cat was the day I made the most important decision of my life. I decided that I was going to grow up to be as different from my mother as it is possible to be.

Leslie's funny comments make the opening anecdote humorous even though it isn't, of itself, a funny story.

5. It is easy in first person to stay in your main character's point of view. If you write in third person, it is possible to tell your story through any or all characters on the page, and this can get confusing, for writer and reader alike. First person confines the writer to one character, all the time. If Leslie is telling her own story, it is clear she can tell only what she herself knows.

To sum up, using a first-person narrator often seems like the easiest approach to take, but it can be the hardest. There may, however, be good reasons for you to choose first person for your story. The decision will have to do partly with the kind of story you are writing. Partly, it will depend on what feels good to you.

Third Person: Disadvantages

A story told in the third person goes like this:

Jeremy James was the luckiest boy in his entire village. His parents, you see, were the village bakers, and every day of the year Jeremy James had biscuits and buns, cream puffs and scones, tortes layered with jelly and puddings bulging with fruit.

But the best time of all to be the bakers' son was just before Christmas, because that was when Jeremy James' papa and mama made gingerbread.
(From my short story
"Jeremy James and the Ginger Bear")

Third person is the more traditional way of telling a story. It does, however, present some challenges, especially to a beginning writer.

1. Often, writers learning to use third person have trouble moving inside the main character to reveal thoughts and feelings.   It isn't difficult to do, but most people have to practice before the technique comes easily. I see more stories fail because the writers don't get inside their main character than for any other reason. (I will say more about handling thought in Chapter 9.)

2. Many beginning writers have difficulty limiting their point of view to their main character when they use third person.   They skip around from character to character. They pop in and out of different people's thoughts and reveal information the main character doesn't know.

Some stories by professional writers do this intentionally. They are written from an omniscient (all-knowing) point of view. This allows the reader to know anything the author chooses to tell.

Many fairy tales are written in this way. The moment you hear the words *Once upon a time,* you know that there is an invisible storyteller narrating the story and that he or she knows everything about everybody.

The lasting popularity of stories such as "Jack and the Beanstalk" and "Rapunzel" proves that the invisible storyteller approach works. But this kind of story usually does leave out an important dimension of modern fiction: the experience of moving inside another human being, looking out through that person's eyes, hearing with that person's ears, sharing that person's thoughts and feelings.

Some of the more complex adult fiction may also be written from an omniscient point of view. In this kind of fiction, however, the reader shares the inner lives of many characters instead of simply following the outer story as it is told. Betsy Byars, an author who writes for young people, frequently uses this technique, too. Look at her novels *Night Swimmers* and *The Glory Girl,* for instance.

Another way of writing from an omniscient point of view is to use different characters to present different sections of the story. In this shifting point of view, the reader moves from being deeply inside one person to being deeply inside another. This gives the author the opportunity to show the same event from different perspectives. Natalie Babbitt's *Tuck Everlasting* is written in this way. My own *Tangled Butterfly* is, as well.

I strongly recommend, however, that beginning writers tell their story only through the main character, even in third person. This is called a third-person limited point of view. You let your readers know what your main character knows, nothing more. By moving in close to your main character, the readers will feel with him and be deeply connected with his story.

> *Michael laid down the .22, carefully, slowly, and took the pigeon, still warm and somehow boneless. He looked from Kari to the blood oozing onto the multicolored feathers. A few drops puddled in his hand. His father's hands had been bloody, too, after he had started to clean the buck. His father's hands had dripped blood, and still he had laughed.*
>
> *But Michael looked down at the warm color gathering in his palm, and something deep inside him turned over.*
>
> (From *Face to Face*)

Notice how you are seeing everything through Michael's eyes, even feeling it with his skin. Notice, too, how what he is experiencing in the present moment is made richer by his emotions and his memories. All of it is woven together, as happens in our experience of real life.

Staying in your character's point of view is not difficult. It just requires that you yourself see the story through your main character's eyes and thoughts and feelings. I always write as though my point-of-view character were between me and the page. Everything I know must pass through him. For most writers, however, that sense takes time to develop . . . especially in third person.

Third Person: Advantages

Working in third person has several advantages for a writer.

1. Probably the biggest advantage is that third person is traditional. It is the way people expect a story to be written. As we settle back to listen when we hear *Once upon a time . . . ,* a third-person voice draws us in. It signals, Here comes a story!

2. In third person, most writers, even beginning writers, have little difficulty moving directly into action. The point of reading fiction (or watching a play or movie) is to live through the action with the characters. We feel with them whatever it is they feel. And this doesn't happen because someone tells us about the events. It happens because the writer dramatizes them, takes the reader through them along with the characters. This is true in either first or third person, but most writers write action more easily in third.

3. There are no limits on your language in third person. You can write about a three-year-old or about a lion in your own language, not theirs. You don't have to make your story sound as though someone other than you is telling it.

Making Your Choice

Having considered all this, you still may not be sure whether first or third person is best for you and for your story. (Some writers do nearly all their work in one manner. Many shift between first and third according to the demands of each story.)

It may help you to think about the stories you most like to read. How are they written? Perhaps nearly all your favorites are written in first person . . . or in third. If you prefer one strongly in your reading, you may also prefer to write that way.

If you don't have a preference, try a few paragraphs, first one way, then the other. Or perhaps you should simply make a choice and start. If the point of view begins to feel wrong as you write, you can always go back and try again with the other.

In any case, this is the last decision for you to make before you begin writing the story itself.

It's time to begin!

At Last . . . The Beginning

If you have gone through all the steps I have suggested up to this point, you are probably impatient to begin. Most people don't realize that writing a story takes so much preparation. Whatever happened to inspiration, some of you may be asking? Doesn't an idea for a story ever arrive whole, ready to be written?

There are times when writers are able to begin writing without going through the steps we have just followed. Occasionally, a complete story actually does come in an instant, like a light bulb going on in a cartoon. But those times, even for professional writers, are rare. (And when they happen, the slow process we have discussed comes in later, when the writer has to evaluate and make revisions in the story.) For most of us, however, sitting around waiting for inspiration to strike will leave us sitting for a long time. Perhaps all our lives.

The process we have just been through is a way of calling inspiration up, step by step. It is also a way of organizing it to make it useful. It is unusual for a story to appear suddenly, without planning or coaxing or *work* of any kind. When it does, the writer has probably gone unconsciously through the steps I have outlined here. In any case, even the most sudden inspiration can be checked out against these steps. If the idea is fully developed, the check will go quickly. If it needs more work, you will see where.

But whether you got to this point in a leap or through careful planning, you are now ready to begin writing your story itself. Go back and read over your story plan. Pay special attention to your character sketches in case there are details you might have forgotten. Then close your notebook and put it aside.

Begin with fresh, loose-leaf paper. Or if you are fortunate enough to be able to write at a computer with a word processing program, sit down to that. Word processors are wonderful tools, and most professional writers use them these days. They take the physical labor out of writing. But millions of stories were written before word processors were ever thought of. I wrote my first two novels on a portable manual typewriter that my parents had given me when I graduated from high school. And I know some writers who still prefer to do at least their first draft by hand.

If you are writing by hand, loose-leaf paper will enable you to move pages around, to rewrite, even to discard. Leave a space, or even two, between lines as you write. If you are typing, set your typewriter on triple space. You will use more paper that way, but you will have room for making changes right on the page instead of having to recopy. You won't want to waste time copying when you could be creating.

The Narrative Hook

The beginning of your story has one primary job: to capture your readers' attention so they will want to go on reading. A narrative hook will do this for you. It will grab your readers and pull them into your story.

What is a narrative hook? Simple. Your story problem.

Your main character's problem gives you a reason for writing your story. It will also give your readers reason to read it. They will read to find out whether the main character manages to get what he wants. Whether the girl escapes being eaten by the tiger. Whether the monster finds a friend. Whether the old man discovers the treasure.

Reveal your main character's problem (at least a strong hint of it) in the first paragraph, even the first sentence, and you will catch your readers' attention. Always keep that problem up front, and they will keep on reading.

Sample the openings of novels or short stories one after the other. What catches your attention? Isn't it the story problem every time? How long does it take for the writer to let you know what the problem is?

Occasionally, there is some reason why the real problem of your story can't begin until later. Then you will need to begin with a minor problem which will lead to the main one. For instance, consider a story in which a boy on a camping trip gets lost in the woods. The problem is finding his way back to camp.

To start with the story problem, you could open with the moment when he realizes he doesn't known how to get back to camp. But that might leave you with too much background to fill in. (How did he get where he is? Why is he alone? How much experience does he have in dealing with wilderness?) Thus, you may want to begin earlier than that. You could, for instance, open with the boy arguing with another camper about who is the best woodsman. That conflict could lead to his doing something foolish and getting lost. Or it could lead to someone else setting him up to get lost. Notice, though, that he would still be facing a problem of some kind from the first moment.

So the narrative hook that you will offer at the opening of your story is either the main story problem or a lesser problem that will lead to the main one. Whichever it is, the problem should be linked to your main character and you should give the readers some idea of what is causing it.

The first sentence of my novel *Shelter from the Wind* is, *Stacy slammed the door behind her.* When you read that line, you know — or can guess — that Stacy is angry. Her anger signals that something is wrong. And you go on reading to find out what it is. By the time you have read a page and a half, you have been filled in on all the details. Stacy is angry with her pregnant stepmother and with her father for having married her stepmother. You also know what she is going to do about her anger. She is going to run away to make her father sit up and take notice.

Don't begin by filling the reader in on all the wonderful background you have gathered. No one cares in the first page that your main character went to third grade in another town and that she hates frilly dresses and that she has two little brothers. That is, your readers don't yet care about any of these things unless they are a part of the immediate problem.

This is why I have suggested closing your notebook before you begin. You won't be tempted to copy onto the first page the information you have gathered. Instead, you can start right off with the story's problem and let everything else slip in when the story needs it.

Start with the problem full blown. Start, in fact, very close to the end of your story. Then everything important will be just about to happen, and it will be easy to hold your readers' attention.

In *Shelter from the Wind,* Stacy's father and stepmother have been married for at least a year. And Stacy has known for long time that her stepmother is going to have a baby. But I didn't open the story back where those things happened. I started it at the exact moment when Stacy decides to do something about her situation. She slams the door and runs away.

Open with dialogue, even an argument that lays out the story problem. Or open with strong action — the main character doing something, or someone else doing something to him. Open at a point at which something is happening, because that will make your story active and fun to read. And if your story is fun to read, it should be fun to write as well.

The Four Ws

There is one other task you need to accomplish very early in your story besides getting your readers' attention. You need to clarify the four Ws, almost exactly the way a news story in a daily paper or on television does. *W*ho is the story about? *W*here is it set? *W*hen is it taking place? *W*hat is going on?

1. Who is the story about? This does not mean that you lay out your entire character sketch in the first couple of pages. However, the readers need to understand some basic facts as soon as possible.

If there is more than one character in the opening scene, who is the story about? Which character should we pay the most attention to? And in the simplest terms, who is this person? A boy or a girl? An aardvark or a zebra? A visitor from Neptune or a ghost from ancient Greece?

What age is he or she, at least approximately? If your main character is a child, this information is particularly important. A six-year-old is very different from a sixteen-year-old. This doesn't mean that you need to start by saying, *Heather was sixteen years old.* Mentioning high school or showing her doing something a girl her age would do will give us enough of a clue. Perhaps she is delivering pizzas or planning for a prom.

With adult characters, a general sense of age, old or middle-aged or young, is usually sufficient. You can often clarify that by physical description. Sometimes an adult's role reveals age, too. A bank president is often mature. A mother with a baby is usually young.

2. Where is it set? The kind of detail you need to give about setting depends upon your story. If you are writing about a very young child, it may be enough to identify the setting as Tommy's backyard. Older characters live in a larger world, though. With them, we will need to locate ourselves in Mississippi or in Michigan, in the United States or in Israel.

You can, of course, simply tell your readers where the story is set. However, there are more interesting ways of giving the signal. Mentioning a cold wind off the ocean could help reveal that your story is happening along the coast of Maine. A lime green sky could be a clue that we are on another planet.

3. When is it taking place? If your story happens in the present, you won't need to tell us that. We will assume it. All you will need to reveal is the season if weather is important. If, however, it happens sometime in the past or in the future, signal the time. If readers start out assuming the story is contemporary and then find themselves in the revolutionary war or the year 2100, they may stop reading instead of readjusting their vision.

Referring to a horse and buggy or a spaceship could be a good start. Giving details of clothing often helps, too. A hoopskirt speaks of one time, saddle shoes and circle skirts another, space helmets another. At some point you may want to tell what year it is, but find a way to slip that in naturally.

4. What is going on? You have essentially taken care of this question already with your narrative hook. Letting your readers know your main character's problem reveals what is happening. But make sure that you have given your readers enough information for clarity. Confusion creates frustration, not story tension.

First Impressions

When we are first learning to dress and to comb our hair, we are all told how important first impressions are. Most human beings make quick judgments about the people they meet — or the stories they read — and are reluctant to change them. So it is important to keep the power of first impressions in mind when you begin writing your story.

This means setting a tone which lets your readers know what kind of a story to expect. If you start out sounding like you are writing a solemnly realistic story and then shift to comedy or to fantasy halfway through, your readers may not make the shift with you. They may simply quit reading.

First impressions are equally important when considering your characters, especially your main character. If your readers don't like your main character, they probably won't care about his story problem. And if you want your readers to like your main character, you won't start out by showing him doing something unappealing like whining, stealing, cheating, bullying, or lying. If, however, you first show your main character in a way which makes the readers care about him, then they will be committed to him. Later, they will be apt to follow your character through whatever behavior his story demands.

And Now to Begin

So . . . it is time to start writing your actual story. Remember that the most important words of any piece you write are those you open with. They will draw your readers in or turn them away. They will also create a solid base upon which all the rest of the story will stand . . . or a wobbly one upon which it will teeter.

When you have written enough of the beginning to reveal the story problem and to answer the four Ws, share your opening with someone, or with a group. You can have them read it to themselves or you can read it aloud while they listen.

Sometimes, readers will notice more details, both the points they like and the ones that don't work, when they can read a piece themselves. However, stories are meant to be listened to, not just read silently, and hearing your work spoken can give you (and your readers) a fresh perspective on it.

Check these questions with your readers: What do they think the story problem is? Who is the main character who has the problem? Where is the story happening? When is it happening? And the most important question of all, After reading just this far, do they want to go on reading? Why or why not?

If you find that your readers are confused about some points, go back and clarify. If your story simply isn't moving, find another place to begin. You may have to write the opening several times before it works . . . for you and your readers.

Writers often write their way into their stories, telling

far more than the reader needs to get the story under way. If that is what you find yourself doing, don't worry about it. Let it happen; then go back and decide where the real story begins. Lop the rest off. Don't throw it away, though. You may need parts of it later. In any case, nothing that you write is ever lost, whether it finds its way into your story or not. It all helps *you* know your story better.

Remember that the opening of your story is usually the most difficult part to write . . . as well as being the most important. So take your time. If you can get the beginning to work, the rest often will follow like water in a freshly dug channel.

Something to Talk About . . . Dialogue

Chapters 9, 10, and 11 deal with dialogue, story tension, and endings. You can use these chapters in different ways. You may want to read through them before you write any more of your story. They will give you important information about technique. Or you may want to put the book aside, finish your story, and then return to these chapters as a guideline for revising, for making changes to improve and strengthen your story.

You can, of course, do both. You may want to read these chapters before you write and return to them again when you are doing revisions.

*

Listen to conversations — on television, among your family and friends, in your classroom. How much can you discover about people by what they say? A woman who talks about money constantly may be worried about being able to pay her bills. Or she may be letting everyone know how much she has. A boy who is constantly threatening to beat someone up may be scared. Or perhaps he believes that strength is his only virtue.

What about the way people speak? We communicate much of our meaning with voice, facial expression, gestures. I can say "Come here" to you in a way that makes you want to go the other way. Or I can make it sound and feel like an invitation to something special.

Your characters will reveal themselves through dialogue, too. And they will affect one another — and the readers — by the way they talk.

Many of the writing techniques you will use in telling a story are ones you have used in other kinds of writing. You have, I am sure, written descriptions in the past. When you write a letter telling your grandparents what you got for Christmas, you are describing. You are describing, too, when you write a composition telling about your room or your dog or a sunset.

You have written narration, too. Have your teachers ever assigned a composition on a topic such as "What I did on my summer vacation"? What you wrote in response was narration — telling events in a summing-up kind of way.

But you may not have written dialogue, and dialogue is an important part of stories.

Uses of Dialogue

Conversations occur in stories because, of course, they occur in life. Your story may come from your imagination, but it will always imitate life. In real life, however, most of us do a lot of talking that no one would want to read. We talk about what we saw on television or complain about our aches and pains or tell jokes everyone has heard before. Sometimes we talk to hear our own voices. We stammer, repeat ourselves, say "um." That kind of conversation won't do much for your story. And besides, think how boring it would be to write!

In stories, dialogue serves at least one of three important functions. In the best writing, it accomplishes all three at the same time.

1. Dialogue gives the reader information.
"I know I'm supposed to like to hunt," the cat said, "but the truth is I find the practice quite disgusting. I nibbled a mouse's tail once, but it tasted like rubber bands."

2. Dialogue reveals character.
Jason turned around, clenching his fists. "You gonna make me? You and who else?"

3. Dialogue moves your story forward.
"There's gold out there. I know there is. And I'm the one who's going to find it first!"

There is a test for any patch of conversation, or for any other unit in your story, for that matter. Could you take it out and leave the story unchanged? If you could, it probably doesn't belong there. But if dialogue is performing one or more of the functions just mentioned, your story won't be able to do without it.

Punctuating Conversation

I have taught fiction writing for many years, and I find that many people have difficulty punctuating dialogue properly. There are three simple rules that will make it quite easy, though.

1. Every time a new person speaks, even if the last has said nothing more than, "Oh!" begin a new paragraph. That way, the paragraphing itself lets the reader know to expect a new voice.

> *"What is your name?"*
> *"Jennifer Bradley."*
> *"Could you possibly be related to the Bradleys who own the big department store downtown?"*

2. Separate the dialogue from the tag (the *he* or *she said* that identifies the speaker) with a comma, not a period. Use a question mark or exclamation mark when it is needed.

> *"Tom Bradley is my uncle,"* she said.
> Or, *"Do you know Tom Bradley?"* she asked.
> Or, *"Tom Bradley!"* she exclaimed.

This rule applies no matter where the tag falls.

> *She said, "Tom Bradley is my uncle."*
> Or, *"Tom Bradley is my uncle,"* she said, *"my father's brother."*

THIS IS INCORRECT: *"Tom Bradley is my uncle."* *she said.* Notice how using a period after *uncle* leaves the *she said* dangling, as though it doesn't belong anywhere.

3. If a sentence of description replaces the tag, each full sentence should stand alone.

"Tom Bradley is my uncle." Jennifer turned to stare at the stranger. "He's my father's brother."

Identifying the Speaker

Most lines of dialogue will need identification for the readers to know who has spoken.

"I love you," the elephant said. "Will you be my wife?"
"You love me?" the mouse squeaked.

When you have only two characters on the scene, however, the start of a new paragraph alone can sometimes be enough to let us know the other person is talking.

"Karen, watch out! That tree is falling!"
"Oh! Help me!"

If we know this scene is happening between Karen and a boy named Tom, when someone says "Karen" we know it must be Tom. And when someone replies, it has to be Karen. Identification tags aren't needed every single time.

Rhythm

Vary the placement of tags to keep the rhythm of your writing flowing. A conversation written like this will sound stilted:

> *"I saw you downtown yesterday," Butch said.*
> *"Did you really? Where was I?" Amy said.*
> *"Near the Seven-Eleven store," Butch said.*
> *"But I wasn't anywhere near there. You must have mistaken someone else for me," Amy said.*

Simply moving the *Butch said* and *Amy said* to different positions in the sentence would make this passage read better.

> *"I saw you downtown yesterday," Butch said.*
> *"Did you really?" Amy said. "Where was I?"*
> *"Near the Seven-Eleven store," Butch said.*
> *Amy said, "But I wasn't anywhere near there. You must have mistaken someone else for me."*

Varying the use of the word *said* can help the flow as well. Now, *said* is a perfectly good word. You don't want to start replacing it with a lot of words that call attention to themselves: *screamed, blubbered, panted, hissed, roared.* There are moments for using strongly descriptive verbs like these to indicate the way dialogue is spoken, but they are rare. Also, be careful about those verbs which may describe something the speaker is doing, but don't describe the manner of speech. Words are not laughed or smiled or clapped or flung or dropped or pouted. They are spoken.

Mostly, the dialogue itself and the situation in which it is spoken will let the readers know how it is spoken. But there are other kinds of neutral verbs — *asked, replied, told, questioned.* They will give variety and help with the flow.

> *"I saw you downtown yesterday," Butch said.*
> *"Did you really?" Amy asked. "Where was I?"*
> *"Near the Seven-Eleven store," Butch told her.*
> *Amy replied, "But I wasn't anywhere near there. You must have mistaken someone else for me."*

Make Your Dialogue Work for You

Instead of letting dialogue just stand by itself, you can make description a part of your tags. You can describe what is going on, how the main character is feeling, what she is thinking. Your readers will get a much fuller picture that way. Using such an approach, you might make the dialogue we just read sound like this.

> *"I saw you downtown yesterday," Butch said. He was leering in an unpleasant way.*
> *Amy studied his face. He seemed to be accusing her of something. "Did you really? Where was I?"*
> *Butch hesitated. "Near the Seven-Eleven store."*
> *"But I wasn't anywhere near there," Amy replied, suddenly relieved. "You must have mistaken someone else for me."*

Notice that by the time we have layered in the further information, the dialogue flows better, too. It is also performing all three of the functions mentioned earlier. It is giving information. It is revealing both of your characters. And it is moving the story forward.

Revealing Thought

I mentioned earlier how important it is to move inside your main character and to reveal thoughts and feelings. In first person, this is no problem. Your narrator simply tells us what he wants us to know. *A thousand butterflies took flight in my stomach. She was the most beautiful girl I had ever seen.*

In third person, beginning writers often handle thought as though it were dialogue. *My stomach is filled with butterflies, David thought. She's the most beautiful girl I've ever seen.*

There is nothing wrong with that method. It does interrupt the flow of your narration, though. It stands out as dramatically as dialogue does. To avoid slowing your story down, you will probably choose to reveal only the most important thoughts in such a manner.

You can get a lot more of your main character's thoughts and feelings onto the page by letting the narrative tell us what they're like. *A thousand butterflies took flight in David's stomach. She was the most beautiful girl he had ever seen.* And then you can go on from there to say a lot more.

Balance

Dialogue breaks up the look of the page and gives action and power to the writing. Most well-written stories have a good balance between narration and dialogue. If you find yourself writing all narration, stop to examine what you are doing. Aren't there places where dialogue could carry your story? If you find yourself writing nothing but dialogue, that is a problem as well. There must be moments in the scene where you could describe what is going on instead of letting the characters do all the talking.

Dialogue is one of a fiction writer's most important tools. Use it well and your stories will come to life.

Story Tension . . . Keeping Your Readers Hooked

Once your story is under way, your task is to keep your readers turning the pages. That doesn't mean you need to dangle someone off a cliff at the end of every scene or sprinkle murders here and there. It means only that you need to keep your main character's — and your readers' — attention focused on the story problem. Then story tension will be maintained.

Another word for *story tension* is *suspense*. Some stories, very strong in story tension, are called suspense stories, but suspense is an important part of every kind of story.

Problem As Tension

The question you want your readers to ask is, What happens next? And it is your main character's struggle to solve his problem that will keep them asking that.

Your main character must stay active. He must be trying, always, to move toward his goal. And he needs to continue to feel strongly about the problem he is trying to resolve.

Do you want to let us know something about your character's history? Get the story under way first and fill in the history only when your readers need to understand more. If you are writing a story about a monster who wants a friend, don't stop your story to tell us how lonely the monster is. Let him tell the princess he has captured how long he has been alone as we worry about her fate. Or let us know about his eating all his previous visitors as we see him planning a party to attract new "friends."

I think of my main character's problem as a rope stretching from the beginning of the story to the end. I never drop the rope, nor do I hang things from it like a clothesline. Rather, I try to weave every part of the story in with it.

You can test each scene in your story with two questions: (1) Is this scene part of your main character's struggle to solve his problem? If your story is about a lonely monster who wants a friend, then a scene in which he does nothing but eat supper doesn't belong. But perhaps while he is eating supper, he chases away all the smaller creatures who try to share his meal. Then the scene is part of the story problem. It lets us see at least one of the reasons the monster is without friends.

(2) Is the main character or his situation changed by what happens in this scene? If the monster sets off to

the palace to make friends with the princess, we expect something important to happen. But what if, after walking for miles, he suddenly decides to return home? The monster hasn't resolved his problem. He hasn't learned anything. We will wonder why he (or we) bothered to set off for the palace in the first place.

If the monster travels long and hard only to be turned away from the palace door, that scene probably belongs in your story. The rejection will change the monster and the direction of the story. It will prompt him either to try to approach the princess in some other way or to find another kind of friend.

Keep your main character moving forward, trying to solve his problem, and story tension will remain high. You will keep your readers' attention as well.

Pacing

Pacing also helps keep your story tension strong. We often have little choice about pacing in our everyday lives. Math class, if you don't like math, seems to last all day. An exciting basketball game seems to be over in minutes. In writing fiction, we are in charge of the way time moves. We can pass quickly over what is unimportant, or even skip it entirely. Then we can stretch out the events we and our readers care about.

The number of words you use to write about a certain event won't depend upon how much time it takes to happen. It will depend on how important that moment is to the story.

It may take your main character only a few seconds

to pick up a gun and shoot a burglar. Those few seconds are important, however. They must be presented in careful detail. If you write only, *He shot the burglar,* we don't have time to feel the action. Describe the moment so we can follow every move, breathlessly.

> *John picked up the pistol. It felt cold in his hand and heavy, heavier than he had expected anything so small to be. He stepped behind the door, pressing his back against the rough wall, holding his breath. Silence.*
>
> *Peering through the crack at the back of the door, he could make out a shadowy figure in the next room. The dark shape moved, picked something up, set it down. That would be his man. It must be. Slowly he raised the gun and . . .*

Beginning writers often give every moment in their stories the same weight. When I was writing my first novel, I used to ask myself, What would my main character do next? Eat dinner? Take a walk? Talk to someone? After I'd had more experience writing fiction, I discovered it was the wrong question. The right question is, What *important* thing would my main character do next *to try to solve her problem?*

You can leave out most tooth brushing, trips to the bathroom, meals, naps, automobile rides, etc. What matters is the action, thoughts, feelings, that will change the outcome of the story.

Consider a story in which a fairy godmother named Cecily has lost her magic wand. You won't start by having Cecily wake up in the morning, brush her teeth, dress, eat breakfast, and then, finally, look for her wand. You'll have her looking for the wand in the first paragraph. And then, if she decides to visit a witch to get help in recovering the lost wand, you won't follow her steps to the witch's cave. That is, not unless something important happens along the way. Instead, you'll summarize her journey and begin writing in detail again when she arrives at the cave.

> *She traveled for many miles. She traveled for many days. She traveled until she arrived at the witch's cave.*

In a longer story, scene breaks can be a good way to leave out unimportant time. When you want to make a leap to the next event, leave a space on the page and begin again.

I could end the first scene of the story just described like this:

> *Cecily's magic wand was gone. There was no question about it. And no one had the power to locate lost objects except Rilda, the meanest witch in the entire kingdom.*

Then after leaving a few empty lines on the page, I could begin the next scene as follows:

> *Cecily stood outside Rilda's dark cave. A smell — it could have been a mixture of skunk, rotten eggs, and dirty socks — wafted from the interior. But she*

put one hand over her nose and stepped closer. However bad it was, she wasn't going to leave without talking to the witch.

Scenes are more complicated to handle than summarizing unimportant action. Each scene needs to draw us in and explain where we are much as the beginning of a story does. It also needs to end on a strong note that will make us want to hurry on to the next scene. Too many scene breaks can make the movement of your story choppy. Too few can leave you describing action that isn't interesting or crucial to your story.

Take note of scenes when you read a short story or a novel. Notice when writers summarize unimportant action or passing time. Notice when they allow time to pass in a blank space on the page. Be aware of scenes in films as well. When the camera fades out and fades in again on a new place or another time, that is a new scene. Ask yourself why the scene shifted, why the story isn't told in one solid stream. As you get a feeling for this in other people's stories, you will understand better how to use scenes in your own.

You will find it easier to follow the movement of time through your story if you attempt to cover as little time as possible. This is another reason for starting the action very close to the end of your story. It is another reason, too, for writing short stories, not novels, when you are first learning. Simply managing the movement through time in a longer work can be a complex task.

Making Your Readers Care

Finally, a tightly drawn story and good pacing alone can't create tension. Most tension stems from the readers' caring about the main character. The way to get them to care is to let them worry, right along with the main character, about his problem. When the readers share his thoughts and feelings, they will understand how important his problem is.

You don't have to like eating worms yourself to worry along with a starving robin who must find worms for her breakfast. At least, you don't have to if you care about the robin. So one of the primary ways of keeping your story tense for your readers is to keep it tense for your main character. Then let your readers feel what he is feeling.

That means you must always be aware of what your main character is thinking, feeling, wanting. You must also know how the world looks, smells, sounds, tastes, and feels to his touch. Good writing uses the senses, all of them. Good fiction writing uses them from inside your main character.

If you write, *Ben was scared,* your readers won't share his fear.

But they will if you get inside him and describe how he feels. *Ben's knees went soft, and there was a taste like old pennies in the back of his mouth.*

The magic that makes fiction work in a way no other kind of writing can is the readers' experience of moving inside the main character, almost of becoming that other person. To give them that, you must first move inside that character yourself and feel the tension of his problem.

"I loved your story. In fact, I couldn't put it down!" That's what every fiction writer longs to hear. And if you get a strong start and keep up the story tension, your readers will be saying it to *you*!

CHAPTER
11

Endings . . .
Expected and Surprising

For me, the most satisfying part of creating any story is writing the ending. It isn't simply that I love being finished, though that is part of it. (And I continue to enjoy the "Done, at last!" feeling with each draft.) Rather, I am writing the entire story because I want to write the ending. My goal is that final scene in which the character either gets what she wants or changes in some way. In that moment, my main character's triumph becomes mine.

You should have known your ending from early in the planning stage, but there are pitfalls to watch out for when you come to write the final scene. We'll take a look at some of these now.

Surprise!

Some writers (and some readers) love surprise endings. And such endings are fine if the writer can make them satisfying and believable as well as surprising. Actually, every ending should have at least some small element of surprise. At the very least, it shouldn't be totally predictable.

For any ending, however, but especially a surprise ending, there must be preparation from the first line. It must be inevitable as well as surprising. The readers' first reaction will be, "Oh!" That should be followed immediately by, "But of course! It had to be that way. Why didn't I figure it out?"

Perhaps you are writing a story in which the surprise is that the "friend" the main character has been talking to the whole time is actually a dog. To make that ending work, you can't simply let us know the truth in the final lines. You will need to give many hints about the secondary character's dogginess along the way.

The hints must be subtle enough, however, so the readers won't catch on too soon. Often your readers' innocence can let you lay down clear hints that aren't too obvious, so that only when the readers get to the end and learn the truth will the hints make sense. The "friend's" shaking himself when he got out of the water, for instance. His never speaking. His running much faster than the main character. His bringing back a thrown ball instead of tossing it.

A surprise ending should fall into place like the last piece completing a puzzle. It should show the full picture for the first time. And it must satisfy your readers in doing so. If you surprise yourself with an ending, you may surprise your readers, as well. It is very unlikely, though, that you will satisfy them.

People who write mysteries must be able to write

surprise endings. In fact, the idea for a mystery begins with the surprise that makes every other piece fall into place. The story then is built to that moment, giving carefully planned clues. So instead of starting your story plan with the mystery problem, you begin by knowing the solution. If, for instance, you are going to write about a murder, you build your plan around the killer, his method, and his motives. Only then can you lay out — and properly disguise — your clues.

As you have probably decided already, good surprise endings are not easy to write. Remember then, that your readers don't need to be surprised to be satisfied. In fact, most of the best story endings rely very little on surprise.

Coincidence

"If you kill your main character off at the end of your story by having him hit by a truck, you have just flunked." That's a warning I used to give my writing students when I was a high school English teacher.

What's wrong with sudden death as the resolution of a story? Usually it is too coincidental, too convenient for the author . . . and too dissatisfying for the readers. Unless, of course, the death is prepared for. How could you prepare for death by truck? Perhaps by letting us see how careless the villain is. Or by showing earlier in the story that someone who drives a truck is out to get him. Or even by letting us see that he really wants to die. If you did one of these things, the death at the end of the story would no longer be coincidental.

We all experience coincidence in our lives, almost

daily. Peas and hamburger glop for school lunch; peas and hamburger glop for supper at home. Saying exactly the same words as your best friend at exactly the same time. Finding that you and a girl you despise have shown up at the dance in identical dresses. But what makes these matters coincidence is that we know no one is behind them. They just happen.

Coincidence in stories is different, though. Your readers always know that you, the author, are behind your story, moving the events. Little coincidences can appear in stories without causing problems. (A boy goes to the mall and just happens to bump into his best friend.)

Any coincidence that helps you work out your plot will make your readers suspicious, however. (The friend's being there gives the boy a chance to borrow the money he needs.)

A coincidence that solves the entire story problem at the end will leave your readers especially dissatisfied. (Because he can borrow the money, the boy pays for the item he stole and escapes being apprehended by the security guards.)

Readers will be left asking, But what would have happened if the coincidence hadn't occurred? The co-incidence, not the main character himself, has solved the story problem.

The Trite Ending

Some endings have been used so many times that they no longer work for the readers, no matter how well they are written.

Probably the most obvious example of a trite ending is having your main character wake up to discover that everything that just happened was only a dream. The first thousand stories that ended this way, including *Alice's Adventures in Wonderland,* were probably fine. But this ending has become trite over the years.

So has the character's returning from some fantasy adventure to find that no time has passed. Or the discovery that the stranger in the story is really a long lost twin. Or having the rough, rude villain turn into the story's hero.

Endings that are too happy, in which every loose end is firmly tied, in which all the bad people are thoroughly punished and all the good ones rewarded, can seem trite, as well. They are simply too predictable.

There are no entirely fresh ideas. Every story is probably similar to others that were written earlier. But some ideas are definitely more hackneyed than others. Triteness can be a problem anywhere in your story, but it will call attention to itself particularly in the ending.

Character Is the Key

To avoid coincidence or triteness, keep your main character in charge of solving his own problem. A story solution that comes directly out of who he is, what he wants, and what he does to get it will work.

Above all, don't let someone else or some external force solve the problem for your main character at the end. That's easy to do. The mother robin explains to the hungry baby robin that he's digging for worms in the wrong place. Worms don't live in concrete sidewalks or on rooftops or beneath bicycle seats. The ghost who is afraid of the dark is given a flashlight by the woman he has scared. A tornado blows away the school the night before the boy must take the chemistry test he isn't prepared for.

The baby robin needs to discover a source of worms for himself. Perhaps he might do it by paying attention for the first time to where the other robins are searching. The ghost needs to get over his fear of the dark or find his own source of safety. The boy needs to find some way of preparing for the test . . . or decide not to cheat because his own integrity is more important than his grade.

One of the reasons we read fiction is to see people solve their own problems. Too often in our own lives we feel stuck, unable to change anything. So we turn to stories to see someone else struggle . . . and succeed. That doesn't mean the main character can't have any kind of help. But the solution must finally be his own.

When You Are Finished

So you've done it! You have planned a story and you have written it, beginning to end. Your story may be three pages long or thirty. It has probably taken you at least two or three weeks to plan and write. Perhaps it has taken more if you have had to work in short bursts or your story is especially complicated. It has also required a lot of thought and effort, but I hope you enjoyed doing it, too. And just think! You are an author now. Congratulations!

Give yourself some time to enjoy what you have done. Put your story aside and go play some video games or read a good book or plan a party. And then, when you are ready to think about your story again, take it out and read it. Enjoy it. But ask yourself, is there any way you might make it even better?

Then, if you want your story to be the very best it can be, turn to the next chapter and begin thinking about revising.

Just When You Thought You Were Done . . . Revising

Many people enjoy writing. Not many like revising — at least in the beginning. However, if you want others to enjoy reading what you write, you *must* learn to revise.

The difficulty most people have learning to revise fully and deeply is another important reason for beginning with short stories, not novels. Starting over on page one to rework a ten-page short story does not seem too hard. To do the same with a one-hundred-fifty-page novel is a formidable task, however.

I earn my living writing fiction, but I spend far, far more of my time revising than I do writing the original draft. In fact, when people ask how many times I rewrote a particular story, I can't tell them. I revise so much that I lose count.

There was a time, though, when I *hated* the idea of revising. I believed that every word I put on the page was gold — or at least silver. Once it was down I wanted only to admire its shine. Of course, I wanted everyone else to admire the shine, too.

I have learned to revise, however. In fact, I have come to like reworking my stories. When I am writing a first draft, there is nothing I can compare my work with . . . except all the fine literature ever written. Thinking of that as I struggle with a new story can be acutely discouraging.

When I am revising, though, I can compare my work with itself. Seeing my story growing stronger, clearer, better, thrills me. My writing is improving, and that is, finally, all that matters.

Remember the image I used in the introduction? That learning to write takes the same hard work as learning to play a musical instrument or to ski? Those skills you gain through practice. You will learn to write the same way. And there is only one kind of practice better than writing a new story. That is returning to a story you have already written and revising it.

It is even possible to enjoy revising. The key is never to think of it as fixing something you did wrong the first time. Rather, think of it as improving something you already love. Stories are created in layers, as I've said before. Certainly your story plan developed that way. Good writing happens the same way.

A test before you begin is important, however. Do you like the story you have written? Do you like it well enough to want it to be even better? Some stories simply don't work well enough in the first draft to justify spending more time on them. Or sometimes you may discover that a particular story idea was a mistake. You have lost interest in it as you worked.

If your story still feels important to you, then you will want to make it work for other people the way the first idea worked inside your head.

Re-Vision

I like to think of revision as *seeing new, re-visioning*. And that is what you need to be able to do before you can improve your story from the inside. You must be able to look at it with fresh eyes, to have a new vision of what your story could be. You must be willing to set aside any part of it that is not working and to be open to new ideas that will make your story stronger and better.

My first several drafts of *A Dream of Queens and Castles* involved a girl, a middle child in her busy family, sent to England for the summer with her professor father to get her out of the way. (At least that was how she interpreted her situation.) When I discovered that the emotional base of my character was not working, I had to rethink her situation, even her family, entirely. I ended up with a story about a girl, the only child of a single parent, who is forced to move to England with her professor mother on a year's sabbatical.

Thus, in the planning stage and again during the writing, I examine my entire story from beginning to end many times. What parts are working? What parts aren't? When a new idea comes to mind, does it change what I already know? Would the character I have created really do what I have her do? Does the ending I have planned say what I want to say?

I try to let the questions flow freely, even when I don't want to hear them. Any idea that will improve my story is worth entertaining.

Editing Yourself

Before you can know what you might want to improve upon, you will need some distance from your first draft. One of the mistakes most beginning writers make is to reread their work too much. We fall in love with it and practically memorize our own words. And once those words are memorized, they are nearly impossible to budge from their first form.

So write with as much speed as you can. Do some rereading as you work to keep the flow. Even do some polishing each time you reread. (I'll talk more about polishing in the next chapter.) But keep moving forward. After you have finished a first draft, read it through once to see what you have done and then put it aside.

During this time away, I write other things . . . or I read. Other people's work sends me back to my own with fresh insights. If you have no deadline pressure, stay away from your story for a week or two. The longer it took you to write the first draft, the longer a separation you will need before you can return to it with a fresh eye.

When you do come back to it again, try to read it as though someone else had written it. Would you like it if it weren't yours? What would you like about it? Are there things that don't seem to work? What are they?

Be specific. Don't simply decide that your story is wonderful or terrible. It is probably neither. Decide what you actually like about it and what would make it better. Then you are ready to begin on another draft.

You may find that you need to rethink some aspects of your story plan. Now would be a good time to go back through this book with your first draft in mind. Ask yourself, again, all the questions I have set up along the way. You might even want to go back to your notebook and *write* the answers. That way you aren't sliding over them, thinking you have answered them when you haven't.

If you find there are some aspects of your story you want to replan, use your notebook for that, too. Maybe your main character isn't coming to life. Go back to your character sketch. Have you used what you know? Do you know enough? Do you need to think more deeply about the character's history? Are you clear about what it is that he wants?

Working with Editors

The more experience you have with writing and revising, the better you will get at evaluating your own work. However, every writer needs the objective view only a good editor can give. For professional writers, editors are people who read manuscripts to decide which ones shall be published. Once they make their selections, editors then work with authors to help them improve their stories.

However, an editor doesn't have to be someone who

reads manuscripts professionally. He or she doesn't even need to be a teacher. Your editor can be a fellow writer or a fellow reader.

If you are using this book in school, your classmates will probably be your primary editors. Set up small critique groups. Or if there is time, read your story aloud to the entire class and listen to the comments. If you are writing on your own, find someone who is willing to read your story and comment on it. It can be a friend, a teacher, a librarian, a neighbor. The best readers will be fellow writers. You can help one another with editing suggestions. But any good reader can learn to be a good editor for you.

It isn't always easy to listen to and accept other people's suggestions about your work. However, if you follow these simple rules, the process can be fun.

What to Expect from an Editor

Ask your editor, first, what he likes about your story. No matter how much work might be needed, you always will have done some things well, perhaps remarkably well. It is part of the editor's job to help you see what those things are. That helps you know what to build on.

It can be easier for your editor to pick a story apart than to define what works and why. Talking about what he likes will be an important part of your editor's own learning. It will also help you hear any suggestions he makes later.

Next, ask your editor if he has any suggestions of what you might do to make your story even better.

Don't ask how you should write your story. That's

not part of an editor's job. He should tell you what he doesn't understand, what he doesn't believe, what seems rough or missing or boring or overdone. He should, however, leave it to you to decide how — and if — to fix the problems he points out.

The purpose of an editor is to encourage you and to help your writing grow. Anyone who doesn't do those two things is not a good editor for you.

What to Expect of Yourself

Be sure you are willing to make revisions. If you think your story is perfect as it is, you are wasting others' time by asking for criticism.

Don't argue. Don't defend. Listen. Take notes. Ask questions if you don't understand a comment. Then think about what was said, but do only what seems right for you and your story.

After listening to comments from a good editor (individual or group), you should feel encouraged. You should be full of energy and ready to tackle your story again. You should also have some ideas about where you want to begin. An editor who tells you your story is "wonderful" but has no suggestions about anything more you might do isn't helping you. On the other hand, an editor who leaves you feeling as though you can't write or shouldn't have bothered to try is destructive. If you run up against either of these extremes, find someone else to help you with your work.

Some ties don't create a good basis for an editor-writer relationship. I suspect that few people, young or old, are entirely comfortable hearing editorial criticism from their parents. Their voices have too much authority. Your editors need to be people you respect, but people who don't have too much influence over your life.

Whoever your editors are, though, always remember that this is *your* story. While you want it to work for your readers, you are the only one who can decide what you want it to say. And you are the only one who can write it.

Rewriting

The hardest part about revising can be keeping yourself from slipping into copying your original draft. Often, in order to make sure I am thinking fresh, I put my last draft aside. In fact, I turn it over so I can no longer see it. Then I begin the story or the scene again, keeping in mind what I want to change.

The original is there. I can always look at it again to find a sentence or section that worked well the first time. I copy that in or cut and paste. (Neatness isn't the point until I need a draft someone else can read.) But then I turn it facedown again and go back to work.

If you are writing on a word processor, print your original draft, then set it aside. Start on a fresh screen. If you keep the original in front of you on the screen, you will change words and phrases, but you probably won't revise.

Be creative with your revisions. Be as creative as you were when you were writing your first draft . . . and more so. You will be surprised how much you can discover that you didn't think of the first time around. Keep in mind that this slow development of the story is what writing, at its best, is all about. Grocery lists can be jotted down once and tossed away when their usefulness is over. You want your story to be good enough to keep for a long time.

When you are confident that you have given your story all that you have to give, the next step is to polish the final draft.

The Final Step ...
Polishing

Polishing is exactly what it sounds like. It is working the surface of your story until it shines. While it is not the deeper work of revision, polishing is important in everything you write.

For writing a story by hand, I suggested earlier that you use loose sheets of paper, not the pages bound into your spiral notebook. I also suggested that you leave one or two spaces blank between your lines of writing. If you are typing, set your typewriter on triple space. Working this way leaves you room for polishing without doing a lot of boring recopying.

If you are lucky enough to be writing on a word processor, you don't have to worry about leaving space. The screen allows you to rework a story as many times as you like with no mess. The trick is to save each draft under a slightly different name — STORY.1, STORY.2, etc. That way, until you are certain your changes are an improvement, you can still return to an earlier draft. When you have a final version, save it by name, STORY, and then you can erase the earlier drafts.

Spelling and Punctuation

If you are working on paper, you should have a pencil ready every time you read through your story. Watch for errors in spelling and punctuation, and correct them as you go.

Are spelling and punctuation important? It's a question I am often asked when I visit schools. And my emphatic answer is, *Yes, they are essential.* The purpose of correct spelling and punctuation is not simply to please teachers, though they will do that. It is to make your writing understandable to everyone who shares the English language with you.

What if I were to write a line from my novel *Touch the Moon* this way: *Munseecker taused hys hed bakd up. Dansed in plas but then he ast. Tring too bee noneshallant wie ur thos. Hurses sew shurt ande funie luking?* With some thought, you can probably figure out what I am saying, but it isn't easy, it is? Translation: *Moonseeker tossed his head, backed up, danced in place. But then he asked, trying to be nonchalant, "Why are those horses so short and funny looking?"*

Spelling and punctuation are part of a writer's basic tools. To write without attending to them is like trying to play the piano without learning the notes. You can write the first draft without worrying about mechanics. Getting the story down is what matters then. But when you polish, check such details as spelling and punctuation with care.

The Right Word

Polishing is also the place to challenge each word you have used. Is it *exactly* the right word? With thought, could you come up with a better one? Did the dog *sleep* or was it only a *nap*? Did the boy *sob* or *whimper*?

Are you using too many adjectives, making your sentences clumsy and heavy? *The searing red sun rose over the steaming jungle sending the lithe, chattering monkeys and the multicolored birds high into the cool, green trees.*

Or are you using too few so that we aren't seeing, tasting, smelling, hearing, feeling, your character's world? *John walked into the room where the witch waited. He looked around. He sat down.*

Are your verbs strong and active? *Crept, stumbled, toddled, lurched, galloped, shuffled, ambled, hiked, strolled,* instead of *walked* or *moved*.

Are your nouns precise? A *robin* or a *blue heron* instead of a *bird*. A *skyscraper* or a *log cabin* instead of a *building*.

Watch for clichés, images that are no longer fresh: *babbling brook, cotton-candy clouds, swimming like a fish*. All of those were fine when they were first used. Now we have heard them so often they are flat. If a word automatically attaches itself to another, the combination is probably a cliché. (Can you think of brook without thinking of *babbling*?)

Watch for descriptive words that are so general they don't say anything: *beautiful, pretty, handsome, nice.* Replace them with specific descriptions. *Her hair was the color of pulled taffy.*

Simile and Metaphor

Is your language rich? Creative? Your teachers have, I am sure, talked about simile and metaphor. Those big words are a nuisance to learn for a test, but the reality they represent is important to writing that comes alive on the page.

A simile is a figure of speech in which one thing is compared to another, using the word *like. The enraged cat rose to her toes like a ballerina.* Or, *The dragon held his breath until he puffed up like a great, green balloon, and then he floated away.*

A metaphor is a figure of speech in which two seemingly unlike things are compared directly. *His words were a time bomb. Five minutes after he had spoken, they exploded in my brain.* Or, *The trees were old women, gossiping with one another.*

Flow

Read your story aloud to yourself, slowly. How does it flow? If you have written entirely in short sentences, it will be choppy.

His father's eyes narrowed further. His mouth disappeared into a tight, straight line. He laid the oars on the ground. He moved with meticulous care. He was like someone who chooses to put down something that he is tempted to throw. He walked back toward Michael.

If you have used nothing but long, complex sentences, the story will be hard to follow.

His eyes narrowing further and his mouth disappearing into a tight, straight line, his father laid the oars on the ground and, moving with the meticulous care of someone who chooses to put down something that he is tempted to throw, he walked back toward Michael.

Good writing uses a balance of long and short sentences.

His father's eyes narrowed further. His mouth disappeared into a tight, straight line. He laid the oars on the ground, moving with the meticulous care of someone who chooses to put down something that he is tempted to throw, and walked back toward Michael.

(From *Face to Face*)

Look for awkward sentences, those where your meaning isn't clear. *Rising from the ground with a rush of wings, the cat watched the bird fly away.* (This exemplifies what is known as a dangling modifier. It suggests that the cat rose from the ground with a rush of wings, not the bird.) *Bob and Tommy walk to the store every afternoon, then he buys an ice cream cone.* (We can't tell which of the boys buys the ice cream cone.)

Check for places where you have told more (or less) than your readers will want to hear about something. Are you taking them through events that don't have a bearing on the outcome of the story? Or are you letting important, strong action happen offstage instead of allowing your readers to experience it with the main character?

Recopying: The Last Resort

Use the blank space between lines to make changes. Work in pencil so you can erase. If a page becomes too messy to read, copy the new version on another page. Don't recopy the whole story, though. You will need to do that only when you want someone else to be able to read it.

As you substitute a stronger word for a weak one, improve a description, clarify an awkward sentence, you are training yourself to be a better writer. The first draft of your next story will be better for the polishing you do on this one. And while polishing will always be part of your process, you will start each time from a stronger, more confident place.

Remember that revising and polishing are crucial for those who want their writing to be the best it can be. Professional writers revise and polish constantly. Don't let it be an unpleasant chore, though. Keep it light. Put your story aside when the rewriting gets to feeling too much like punishment.

Writing, revising, and polishing your story may not be easy, but they should be things you enjoy doing. After all, as I said in the beginning, if your story isn't a pleasure to write, what's the point?

A Career as a Fiction Writer

So your story is done. You have planned it, written it, revised and polished it. "Now," elementary and middle school students ask me over and over again, "where can I get my story published?"

It is a question that always dismays me, because I know no one will want to hear the only answer I can give: *You probably can't get it published anywhere.*

After studying the violin for a few months, you wouldn't be ready to audition for a professional orchestra. People study music for years in order to prepare for such an opportunity. In fact, the road to being professional is so arduous that few musicians choose it. Most play for their own pleasure and that of their friends. Yet everyone who writes a first story wants to be published.

The reality is that you probably won't be ready to write for publication for many years. Your own school newspaper or literary magazine would be an exception.

They are created precisely for the purpose of publishing beginning writers. Some national magazines have contests for young writers, and sometimes local newspapers do, as well. But the competition for these is usually very stiff. And a young writer hasn't a chance to compete with adult professionals in the book and magazine markets.

I know that sounds discouraging. It isn't meant to be. There are many reasons for writing that have nothing to do with being published. (Who would require a concert stage in order to enjoy playing the piano?)

Most writers, even most adult writers, will not be published . . . ever. And yet, they will go on writing. Why? Because it's fun to do. Because learning to write is a challenge, like learning to juggle or to play chess. And it gets more interesting with practice. Because forming ideas into words helps us understand ourselves. Because it's a way of sharing our thoughts and feelings with others.

The world accepts every other form of art as a hobby, something people do for their own pleasure. How many people paint pictures without ever expecting to sell one to a museum or show it in a gallery? Writing, even for professional writers, begins as a hobby, too. It begins by being something that the writer does for his or her own pleasure.

Let's return, then, to your story. You have finished it. You have copied off a final draft. Maybe you have even illustrated it. What do you do with it now, if there's little chance that it will be published?

Pass it among your friends. Read it to your family

some evening after supper. As a class project, illustrate and cover and bind your story and donate it to your school library. Or if yours is suitable for younger children, volunteer to read it to a kindergarten class.

Most of all, if you enjoyed writing this story, begin another. For all of us writers, professional and amateur, the real reward lies in the act of writing, not in anything that happens after. Just gathering ideas and seeing them come alive on the page is thrilling. And that you can experience every time you sit down to write.

If You Do Want to Write Professionally

Some of you know, right now, that you want to work toward being professional writers. That's fine. In fact, it's wonderful! I, too, knew I was "going to be a writer" when I was very young. I wasn't quite sure how to get a story down on paper then, but I knew I liked to write . . . school assignments, letters, journals, poems, all of it. And liking to write — along with a lot of doing it, year after year — got me published eventually. It can do the same for you.

Let me tell you what you will have to do to get published. The process isn't mysterious, just lengthy and a bit tedious.

You will begin, of course, with a finished manuscript. It will be one you have worked on long and hard, one which you believe to be truly professional. You will type (or print through a word processor) a clean copy, double spaced, with good margins. You will mail it to a magazine or book publisher who publishes the kind of story you have written. And you will include a stamped, self-addressed envelope for its return.

Then you will wait.

In most large libraries there are several books available that give the addresses of various publishers. They will also give the editors' names and information about the kinds of stories each is looking for. The best known are *The Writer's Handbook* (published by *The Writer*) and *The Writer's Market* (published by *Writer's Digest*). In fact, those two magazines, *The Writer* and *Writer's Digest,* can be excellent learning tools for you in the future. I first subscribed to a writer's magazine in my midteens. And I continued reading them long after I began publishing in my midthirties.

With most publishers, you will probably wait anywhere from six weeks to six months to receive a response. (During this time, you will, of course, be working on another story.) Then one day you will go to your mailbox and find, most likely, that your manuscript has come home. It will have a rejection slip attached. A rejection slip is a note that says, basically, "Thanks, but no thanks."

Usually a rejection slip gives you little or no information about the editor's reasons for not wanting your story. (Editors don't mean to be either unkind or unhelpful. They simply don't have time to be writing teachers.) The editor might think it's the worst piece of writing she has ever seen. She might like it very much but have published something too much like it recently. Or the topic might simply be wrong for her. But you will probably know only one thing for certain. *This* publisher doesn't want your story.

So you will choose another publisher, once more mail your manuscript with its stamped, self-addressed envelope, and go back to waiting . . . and writing. Probably your story will come back to you again, and again you will mail it out. If you are lucky and if your story is good enough, one day you will receive a letter from an editor. "I want to publish your story," it will say.

Usually, however, the letter will continue with, "*But there are some changes I think you should make.*" And if you want that editor to publish your story, you will have to begin revising again. (An editor has an objective view we writers cannot have of our own work, and usually their suggestions are very helpful.)

Sound difficult? It is. Sound discouraging? It can be. If your parents worked this way, they would go to their jobs without getting paid for the next six weeks or six years. At the end of whatever time it took them to finish a project, the boss would say, "Yes, I like it. I'll pay you." Or, "No, thanks. Your work isn't what I'm looking for."

Still, a writer's life is good. I can attest to that. But there are some basic facts about a writing career anyone considering it should know.

The Bad News

It is difficult to get published. As I have already said, getting published is not easy even for adults who have been writing for a long time.

Most book publishers accept less than one manuscript out of each one hundred they receive. However, an unpublished writer's chances aren't even as good as that. Many of the books on any publisher's list are by writers who have published with that company in the past. A new writer's chances (and I am talking about adults who are trying to be professionals) are probably closer to one in a thousand.

The young people's magazine *Cricket,* which you may read, receives close to 15,000 manuscripts a year and publishes about 130. That is less than one in a hundred. *Redbook* receives close to 40,000 unsolicited short-story manuscripts a year. They publish between 30 and 40 in that time. That is less than one in a thousand. So you can see that getting a foot in the publishing door, especially with fiction, isn't easy.

If you do get published, you probably won't be famous. If fame is what you want, you might do better joining a rock band . . . or trying to be a quarterback for a Super Bowl team. Few writers get to be well known. Even those who do aren't apt to be asked for their autographs when they walk down the street.

If you do get published, you probably won't be rich. Magazines pay anywhere from nothing to $5,000 for a story. And far more pay nothing or very little than pay $5,000.

Books are usually sold on the royalty system. Traditionally, the writer earns 10 percent of the price of the book. That means each time a copy of a book sells for $15.00, the author earns $1.50. Royalties (and prices) on paperbacks are much lower. It is only the rare book that sells in large enough quantities to earn much for the writer.

People often have an image of writers as being

wealthy. When I visit schools, students want to know if I arrived in a limousine. The truth is, I have never ridden in a limousine in my life. For the first fifteen years of my writing career, I was not able even to support myself with my work. Now I am. Actually, I support myself with a combination of writing, lecturing, and some teaching. I also drive a modest and rapidly aging car. Most writers must have jobs in addition to their writing, especially if they have families dependent on them.

A writer has to learn alone and work alone. There are many helpful classes, in school and out, to help writers on their way. Finally, however, you must teach yourself to write. You learn by sitting alone and writing . . . and writing . . . and writing. And if you stay with it, you will continue to work alone for your entire career. If being alone much of the time isn't for you, then you will probably want to think about another kind of work.

The Good News

So you know all that, but you still want a career as a writer. You have much to look forward to.

Getting published becomes easier after you have a toe in the door. While my editor doesn't automatically accept anything I write, I know he looks forward to seeing my manuscripts. And he is willing to work long and hard to help me get a manuscript right for publication. Thus, having my work published becomes easier for me all the time.

Also, it is important to know that many of the thousands of manuscripts that will reach an editor's desk at the same time as yours won't be able to compete with it. They will be carelessly and poorly written. Your story will stand out if it is really good. And if you work hard, learn how to revise deeply, know the field you are writing for, and research the publisher's requirements, your chances will be even better.

You may actually get to be famous . . . or you may prefer a simpler life anyway. I love to met people who have read my stories or to get letters from them. However, I haven't the slightest desire to be recognized as "somebody" when I run to the grocery store in my oldest sweat suit. It is having my books, not my face, recognized that matters to me. And even very famous writers can usually keep their faces (and their lives) quite private.

Some writers do get rich. Few teachers, factory workers, retail clerks, waiters, police officers, or pharmacists do.

Working alone may be fine for you. I love being with my family, having dinner with friends, meeting new people. When I am working, however, I *love* being alone. I like setting my own challenges and my own goals and teaching myself what I need to know.

I work alone, and yet I have the privilege of reaching out and touching other people through my words. I constantly meet readers and receive their letters letting me know that has happened. This is, for me, the best of all possible worlds.

You can be in charge of your own work life. No one tells me when to begin working or when to quit. No one even tells me what to work on. That is all up to me. I can go to work without ever leaving my comfortable home. I can go out and walk in the morning sun, then work later in the day if I choose. I can take a day off in the middle of the week and then work on Saturday . . . or not work on Saturday. When I had children in school, I was able to be there, still working, when they came home at the end of the day. I set my own schedule and answer only to myself.

Most important of all, you can do work you love. Too few people are able to earn their living doing what they truly love. My father used to say, "The reason they call it work is because you don't like doing it. If you liked it, no one would pay you." And that is, I'm afraid, true for many, many people.

Ask your parents and other adults you know: "If you could do any work at all, would you be doing what you are now?" You might be surprised at how many will say, "Well, what I really wanted to be was a brain surgeon or a rodeo clown or . . ."

I would continue to write even if my writing didn't earn me a cent, even if no one ever read my stories. I feel very fortunate to be able to make a career of what I would gladly do as a hobby.

It isn't selling a story that makes you a writer. It is picking up a pencil or a pen, sitting down to a typewriter or a word processor, and beginning to build a world with words. If you can do that, and if you can do it with love, you are a writer indeed.

I wish you well.

An Afterword . . .
On Using This Book

Writers often debate as to whether writing can really be taught. Many of us have had mentors, people whose work we admired and who have, perhaps, given us advice and encouragement along the way. However, most professional writers have learned to write simply by writing, day after day, without aid of teachers or even books on writing.

The creation of stories involves both craft (which is primarily what this book deals with) and inspiration. About 90 percent craft and 10 percent inspiration.

The part that is craft can be learned through practice. A teacher or a good how-to-write book can be useful, too, and can make your practice more effective. In fact, learning your writing craft is like learning to use the tools of any trade. Imagine building a house without first learning how to use a hammer!

On the other hand, imagine building a perfect

house and leaving it to stand empty. A story that follows all the steps I have laid out here but that lacks inspiration, energy, passion, would be like that empty house.

The danger of how-to-write books is that they are static. I can present the process I use, the one I have used with many students, but I can't adjust my recommendations to the particular needs of each of my readers.

The suggestions I have made here have worked for many writers and for many stories. Still, there are times when they won't fit the story you are trying to write. I believe that beginners do well to learn to follow the kind of structure I am suggesting before deciding that they know enough to put it aside and try another way. But (and this is a very important *but*) no one can judge whether these suggestions will strengthen or weaken your particular inspiration except you.

Don't use this book as a straitjacket, a set of rules that take the fun out of writing. There is, finally, only one rule that every fiction writer must attend to. That is, you must make your story work for your reader.

No, there is one other rule. You must make it work for yourself first.

So use this book as long as it helps you. Set it aside when it doesn't. If some of the steps I recommend seem tedious or confusing or simply don't lead you anywhere, don't take those steps. Perhaps you will find a use for them on another story. Or perhaps you will find they don't work for you at any time.

To write truly good stories, stories that will satisfy

you as well as your readers, you must do something no writing teacher, no book, no guidelines, can help you with. You must take risks.

Knowing your craft can help you tell a story. But only by taking risks can you make art.

Index

Action: pacing descriptions of, 89–92; vs. narration, 59, 66

Beginnings, 70–77

Career in writing, 118–26
Cause and effect, 52–53
Characters: active, 88–89; appearance of, 23–24, 26–27; caring about, 18, 30, 71–72, 75, 93; changes in, 10, 31, 42–43, 53, 88–89; contradictions in, 31–33; dialogue and, 80, 82, 85; first impressions of, 73–75; history of, 20–21, 88; ideas for, 33–36; knowing from inside, 18–21, 27, 35–36, 44–45, 93–94; motives of, 18–21; naming, 21–22; personality traits of, 29–33; secondary, 25–27, 33; solving own problems, 99–100; stereotyped, 18, 35. *See also* Point of view; Struggle
Clichés, 113
Coincidence, 97–98, 99
Conflict, 3. *See also* Struggle
Conversation. *See* Dialogue
Craft, 127

Description, 60, 113–14;
   of action, 89–92; in dialogue tags, 83–84
Dialogue, 78–79; balance
   of narration with, 86;
   functions of, 80, 85;
   punctuating, 81–82;
   rhythm of, 83; speakers
   identified in, 81–84

Editing, 105–9
Editors, 106–9, 121–22,
   124
Endings, 41–45, 95; char-
   acter as key to, 99–100;
   coincidence and, 97–98,
   99; surprise, 95–97;
   trite, 98–99
Environment, 24–25, 26,
   60, 73–74
Events, importance of, 89–
   92, 116
Experience, writing from,
   13–15, 16, 33–36, 40–
   41

Fame, 123, 125
Feedback, 76, 106–9
Figures of speech, 114
First draft, 69–70. *See also*
   Revising

Formula, 46–56
Four W's, 72–75

Ideas: choosing, 8–16; getting, 3–7, 15, 33–36,
   38–39; importance of,
   to writer, 12–13, 16
Income from writing, 123–
   24, 125
Inspiration, 68–69, 127

Magazines, writers', 121
Mechanics of writing, 81–
   82, 112–13
Metaphor, 114
Motive, 18–21
Mysteries, 96–97

Names of characters, 21–
   22, 26
Narration: balance of dialogue with, 84; vs. action, 59, 66
Narrative book, 70–72
Notebook, 3–7, 13, 18–
   19, 24, 25, 36, 44, 51,
   69, 72, 106
Novel, 3, 55, 102

Observation, 23–24
Openings. *See* Beginnings

Pacing, 89–92
Paper, 69, 111
Parents as editors, 108–9
Physical appearance of characters, 23–24, 26–27
Plot, 46–56; graph of, 51
Point of view, 57, 66–67; first person, 19, 58–62, 85; omniscient, 63–64; third person, 26, 62–66, 85
Polishing, 111–17
Problem. *See* Struggle
Publication, 118–23, 124–25
Publications for writers, 121
Punctuation, 81–82, 112–13

Recopying, 69–70, 109, 111, 116, 120
Rejection slips, 121
Revising, 102–10, 122; beginning of story, 76–77. *See also* Polishing
Risks, 129
Royalties, 123
Rules for fiction writers, 59, 128

Scene breaks, 91–92
Sentences, length of, 114–15; unclear, 115–16
Setting. *See* Environment
Sharing, 76, 106–9, 119–20
Short story, 3, 26, 92, 102
Simile, 114
Situation, 9–10
Solutions, 9, 39, 99–100. *See also* Endings; Struggle
Spelling, 112–13
Stereotypes, 18, 35
Story: circular, 42–43; defined, 2–3; formula, 46–56; linear, 43; suspense, 87
Story plan, 1, 3, 69, 106
Story tension, 60, 75; character as source of, 87–89, 93–94; pacing for, 89–92; struggle as source of, 87–89, 93
Stretching reality, 13–15, 16
Struggle, 2–3, 5–7, 9–22, 16; characters resolving own, 99–100; history of character and, 20–21, 88; importance of to

Struggle (*cont.*)
character, 11–12, 88, 93; as narrative hook, 70–72; personality and, 29–31; plot and, 47–55; secondary characters and, 26; as story tension source, 87–89, 93; theme and, 38–40
Summarizing, 91–92
Suspense. *See* Story tension

Tags, 81–84
Tension. *See* Story tension
Theme, 37–41
Threes, use of, 48–52
Time, 60, 74, 92; skipping over, 89–92; writer's management of, 1–2, 4, 7, 12, 100–101, 105

Tone, 75
Triteness, 98–99, 113
Typing, 69, 111, 120

Verbs, 83–84, 113

"What if," 13–15; 16
Word choice, 113–14
Word processors, 69, 109, 111–12, 120
Working alone, 124, 125–26
Writer, The, 121
Writer's block, 53–55
Writer's Digest, 121
Writer's Handbook, 121
Writer's Market, 121
Writing as career, 118–26
Writing by hand, 69, 109, 111